WHAT GOD'S WORD SAYS ABOUT BULLYING

WHAT GOD'S WORD SAYS ABOUT BULLYING

THE BIBLE PROMISE BOOK® FOR KIDS

Written and compiled by
Janice Thompson

SHILOH kidz
An Imprint of Barbour Publishing, Inc.

Published by Shiloh Kidz, an imprint of Barbour Publishing, Inc., 1810 Barbour Drive, Uhrichsville, Ohio 44683, www.shilohkidz.com

Our mission is to inspire the world with the life-changing message of the Bible.

ecpa Member of the
Evangelical Christian
Publishers Association

Printed in the United States of America.
000217 0320 SP

CONTENTS

INTRODUCTION

God, please help!
Mean people are bullying me and my friends.
What can I do?

When it feels as though the whole world is against you, and *nobody* is treating you right. . .

Somebody is calling you names, and you don't know why.

People are criticizing your looks or your brains or your athletic ability.

One kid seems determined to make you and your friends as miserable as possible.

Whatever it is that turned your day from right-side-up to upside down, God knows and He cares. And He has a lot to say about it in His Word, the Bible.

Did you know that the Bible is full of God's promises just for you? And if you take time to read and think about those promises, even the worst day at school or in the neighborhood can have a wonderful turnaround. It's true!

What God's Word Says about Bullying is over-flowing with words of love from the heavenly Father and the wisdom you need to get through those hard days—with hope in your heart and a smile on your face.

Read on to meet the strong, true Friend who will always be on your side, now and forever!

ANGeR

Bullying and anger just go together, don't they?

Oh sure, if you're being bullied you'll feel a lot of other emotions too: fear, sadness, loneliness, frustration. At some point though, you'll probably get mad as well.

But the bullies themselves are often angry—they're taking out their anger on others.

No wonder the Bible warns us so often against anger. Unless it's dealt with properly, it can really mess people up.

How do you handle anger? Recognize it. Admit you're angry. Then talk to God about it. Ask Him to help you put out the fire. Ask Him to put out the bully's fire. Ask Him for a wise adult to give you a hand. And ask Him for wisdom to deal with difficult people—without anger.

Love does not get angry. Love does not remember the suffering that comes from being hurt by someone.
1 CORINTHIANS 13:5

A man's anger does not allow him to be right with God.
JAMES 1:20

Put out of your life all these things: bad feelings about other people, anger, temper, loud talk, bad talk which hurts other people, and bad feelings which hurt other people.
EPHESIANS 4:31

A gentle answer turns away anger, but a sharp word causes anger.
PROVERBS 15:1

Men who speak against others set a city on fire, but wise men turn away anger.
PROVERBS 29:8

If you are angry, do not let it become sin. Get over your anger before the day is finished.
EPHESIANS 4:26

Put out of your life these things also: anger, bad temper, bad feelings toward others, talk that hurts people, speaking against God, and dirty talk.
COLOSSIANS 3:8

Do not have anything to do with a man given to anger, or go with a man who has a bad temper.
PROVERBS 22:24

I want men everywhere to pray. They should lift up holy hands as they pray. They should not be angry or argue.
1 TIMOTHY 2:8

Do not be quick in spirit to be angry. For anger is in the heart of fools.
ECCLESIASTES 7:9

"But I [the Lord] tell you that whoever is angry with his brother will be guilty and have to suffer for his wrong-doing."
MATTHEW 5:22

My Christian brothers, you know everyone should listen much and speak little. He should be slow to become angry.
JAMES 1:19

Live in peace with each other. Do not act or think with pride. Be happy to be with poor people. Keep yourself from thinking you are so wise.
ROMANS 12:16

He who plants sin will gather trouble, and the heavy stick of his anger will break.
PROVERBS 22:8

"Their anger will be punished, for it is bad. Their bad temper will be punished, for it is bad."
GENESIS 49:7

"The Lord is slow to anger and filled with loving-kindness, forgiving sin and wrong-doing. But He will not let the guilty go without being punished."
NUMBERS 14:18

But You, O Lord, are a God full of love and pity. You are slow to anger and rich in loving-kindness and truth.
PSALM 86:15

Shake with anger and do not sin. When you are on your bed, look into your hearts and be quiet.
PSALM 4:4

The anger of a fool is known at once, but a wise man does not speak when he is spoken against.
PROVERBS 12:16

He who is slow to anger is better than the powerful. And he who rules his spirit is better than he who takes a city.
PROVERBS 16:32

An angry man will suffer punishment. For if you save him from his trouble, you will only have to do it again.
PROVERBS 19:19

The things your sinful old self wants to do are: sex sins, sinful desires, wild living, worshiping false gods, witchcraft, hating, fighting, being jealous, being angry. . . . I told you before and I am telling you again that those who do these things will have no place in the holy nation of God.
GALATIANS 5:19–21

Work to get along with others. Live in peace.
2 CORINTHIANS 13:11

A church leader is God's servant. His life must be so that no one can say anything against him. He should not try to please himself and not be quick to get angry over little things.
TITUS 1:7

As much as you can, live in peace with all men.
ROMANS 12:18

A man's understanding makes him slow to anger. It is to his honor to forgive and forget a wrong done to him.
PROVERBS 19:11

When one is slow to anger, a ruler may be won over. A gentle tongue will break a bone.
PROVERBS 25:15

A gift in secret quiets anger. A gift from the heart quiets strong anger.
PROVERBS 21:14

"I tell you, love those who hate you. Respect and give thanks for those who say bad things to you. Do good to those who hate you. Pray for those who do bad things to you and who make it hard for you. Then you may be the sons of your Father Who is in heaven."
MATTHEW 5:44–45

Do not let yourselves get tired of doing good. If we do not give up, we will get what is coming to us at the right time.
GALATIANS 6:9

Oh God, I'm so angry!
I hate it when people bully me and my friends!
Why do people have to be so mean?

....

Father, please help me to turn my anger into prayer. When I'm mad, may I run straight to You. Send someone to help me—a parent, a friend, or a teacher. Keep me from saying angry words and acting like the bully, Lord. You want me to be like Jesus, who didn't fight back against the people who wanted to kill Him—and even asked You to forgive them. He told me to love my enemies, and pray for the people who mistreat me. So here it is, Father—please show my bully Your love. Help that bully to find peace in You.

CHOICES

Bullying is a choice. You can choose to go along with the crowd and bully someone, or you can choose not to.

So, how do you make better choices? First, decide in your heart to have a "no bullying, no matter what" attitude. Then, don't give in to the temptation when others start picking on people—at school, in your neighborhood, or even at church. (Yes, people sometimes get bullied at church too.)

Choose to step away from the bullies. Choose to help those who are being bullied. Choose to go to an adult when situations get out of hand. Choose to trust that God will take care of you.

Most of all, choose to love—the ones who are being hurt and even the ones doing the hurting.

"Go in through the narrow door. The door is wide and the road is easy that leads to hell. Many people are going through that door. But the door is narrow and the road is hard that leads to life that lasts forever. Few people are finding it."
MATTHEW 7:13–14

There is a way which looks right to a man, but its end is the way of death.
PROVERBS 14:12

The mind of a man plans his way, but the Lord shows him what to do.
PROVERBS 16:9

Your ears will hear a word behind you, saying, "This is the way, walk in it," whenever you turn to the right or to the left.
ISAIAH 30:21

"Let us choose for ourselves what is right. Let us know among ourselves what is good."
JOB 34:4

The last word, after all has been heard, is: Honor God and obey His Laws. This is all that every person must do. For God will judge every act, even everything which is hidden, both good and bad.
ECCLESIASTES 12:13–14

Christian brothers, keep your minds thinking about whatever is true, whatever is respected, whatever is right, whatever is pure, whatever can be loved, and whatever is well thought of. If there is anything good and worth giving thanks for, think about these things.
PHILIPPIANS 4:8

My son, do not forget my teaching. Let your heart keep my words. For they will add to you many days and years of life and peace. Do not let kindness and truth leave you. Tie them around your neck. Write them upon your heart. So you will find favor and good understanding in the eyes of God and man.
PROVERBS 3:1–4

Agree with Him in all your ways, and He will make your paths straight.
PROVERBS 3:6

"If you think it is wrong to serve the Lord, choose today whom you will serve. Choose the gods your fathers worshiped on the other side of the river, or choose the gods of the Amorites in whose land you are living. But as for me and my family, we will serve the Lord."

JOSHUA 24:15

He will eat milk and honey when He knows enough to have nothing to do with wrong-doing and chooses good.

ISAIAH 7:15

You have never been tempted to sin in any different way than other people. God is faithful. He will not allow you to be tempted more than you can take. But when you are tempted, He will make a way for you to keep from falling into sin.

1 CORINTHIANS 10:13

"Be sure you do not do good things in front of others just to be seen by them. If you do, you have no reward from your Father in heaven."

MATTHEW 6:1

Do not be jealous of a man who hurts others, and do not choose any of his ways.
PROVERBS 3:31

If we tell [Christ] our sins, He is faithful and we can depend on Him to forgive us of our sins. He will make our lives clean from all sin.
1 JOHN 1:9

"But you must obey the Lord your God to keep His Laws which are written in this book of the Law. You must turn to the Lord your God with all your heart and soul."
DEUTERONOMY 30:10

You get what is coming to you when you sin. It is death! But God's free gift is life that lasts forever. It is given to us by our Lord Jesus Christ.
ROMANS 6:23

You have tested my heart. You have visited me during the night. You have tested me and have found nothing wrong. I have decided that my mouth will not sin.
PSALM 17:3

Do not let anyone lead you in the wrong way with foolish talk. The anger of God comes on such people because they choose to not obey Him.
EPHESIANS 5:6

So give yourselves to God. Stand against the devil and he will run away from you.
JAMES 4:7

We do not compare ourselves with those who think they are good. They compare themselves with themselves. They decide what they think is good or bad and compare themselves with those ideas. They are foolish.
2 CORINTHIANS 10:12

Look to the Lord and ask for His strength. Look to Him all the time.
1 CHRONICLES 16:11

The Laws of the Lord are right, giving joy to the heart. The Word of the Lord is pure, giving light to the eyes.

Psalm 19:8

You have tested my heart. You have visited me during the night. You have tested me and have found nothing wrong. I have decided that my mouth will not sin.

Psalm 17:3

A wise man will hear and grow in learning. A man of understanding will become able.

Proverbs 1:5

Watch yourselves! You do not want to lose what we have worked for. You want to get what has been promised to you.

2 John 1:8

Teach me Your way, O Lord. I will walk in Your truth. May my heart fear Your name.

Psalm 86:11

*Help me step away, Lord. . .
far, far away!*

. . . .

*It's not easy, Lord, but today I'm choosing to step
away from all bullying. I'll keep my eyes wide open.
I'll be on the watch for kids who are being bullied.
I won't go along with the crowd and I'll make sure
an adult knows if someone is being hurt by others.
Lord, help me to forgive those who are bullying
others—even if they're bullying me. But also
make me brave enough to stand against what they
are doing. Bullying is wrong, Lord. Most of all,
I choose to be like You, Jesus. You love all people,
even those who are different. You don't pick on
people. You're not mean. So I choose Your way.*

COMPASSION

What does it mean to have compassion? When you are compassionate, you care about other people. It means you sympathize with them when they're going through hard times.

It bothers you to see them bullied or ridiculed by others. Your heart hurts when they are hurt. You care. . .a lot.

Not everyone has compassion for others. Some people are self-centered or just downright mean. They're the opposite of compassionate. But God wants you to care about others—especially those who are ridiculed and made fun of.

Why does God care so much about these people? Because He loves them as much as He loves you. . .and He loves you a lot!

You must be kind to each other. Think of the other person. Forgive other people just as God forgave you because of Christ's death on the cross.
EPHESIANS 4:32

When Jesus got out of the boat, He saw many people gathered together. He had loving-pity for them. They were like sheep without a shepherd. He began to teach them many things.
MARK 6:34

God has chosen you. You are holy and loved by Him. Because of this, your new life should be full of loving-pity. You should be kind to others and have no pride. Be gentle and be willing to wait for others. Try to understand other people. Forgive each other. If you have something against someone, forgive him. That is the way the Lord forgave you.
COLOSSIANS 3:12–13

Help each other in troubles and problems. This is the kind of law Christ asks us to obey.
GALATIANS 6:2

[Jesus] had loving-pity for them and healed those who were sick.
MATTHEW 14:14

Last of all, you must share the same thoughts and the same feelings. Love each other with a kind heart and with a mind that has no pride.
1 PETER 3:8

What if a person has enough money to live on and sees his brother in need of food and clothing? If he does not help him, how can the love of God be in him?
1 JOHN 3:17

Then David said, "Is there anyone left of the family of Saul, to whom I may show kindness because of Jonathan?"
2 SAMUEL 9:1

But You, O Lord, are a God full of love and pity. You are slow to anger and rich in loving-kindness and truth.
PSALM 86:15

"Do not say what is wrong in other people's lives. Then other people will not say what is wrong in your life. You will be guilty of the same things you find in others. When you say what is wrong in others, your words will be used to say what is wrong in you."
MATTHEW 7:1–2

It is because of the Lord's loving-kindness that we are not destroyed for His loving-pity never ends. It is new every morning. He is so very faithful.
LAMENTATIONS 3:22–23

The Lord has loving-pity on those who fear Him, as a father has loving-pity on his children.
PSALM 103:13

So the Lord wants to show you kindness. He waits on high to have loving-pity on you. For the Lord is a God of what is right and fair. And good will come to all those who hope in Him.
ISAIAH 30:18

And God said, "I will have My goodness pass in front of you. I will make the name of the Lord known in front of you. I will have loving-kindness and loving-pity for anyone I want to."
Exodus 33:19

"The son got up and went to his father. While he was yet a long way off, his father saw him. The father was full of loving-pity for him. He ran and threw his arms around him and kissed him."
Luke 15:20

Praise the Lord, O my soul. And forget none of His acts of kindness. He forgives all my sins. He heals all my diseases. He saves my life from the grave. He crowns me with loving-kindness and pity.
Psalm 103:2–4

"If the one who hates you is hungry, feed him. If he is thirsty, give him water. If you do that, you will be making him more ashamed of himself."
Romans 12:20

"The Lord of All said, 'Do what is right and be kind and show loving-pity to one another. Do not make it hard for the woman whose husband has died, or the child who has no parents, or the stranger, or the poor. Do not make sinful plans in your hearts against one another.'"
ZECHARIAH 7:9–10

But [God] showed them loving-kindness and forgave their sins. He did not destroy them. He held back His anger many times. He did not let all of His anger loose.
PSALM 78:38

The Lord is loving and right. Yes, our God is full of loving-kindness.
PSALM 116:5

We think of those who stayed true to [God] as happy even though they suffered. You have heard how long Job waited. You have seen what the Lord did for him in the end. The Lord is full of loving-kindness and pity.
JAMES 5:11

O man, He has told you what is good. What does the Lord ask of you but to do what is fair and to love kindness, and to walk without pride with your God?
MICAH 6:8

The Lord is full of loving-pity and kindness. He is slow to anger and has much loving-kindness.
PSALM 103:8

Do not work only for your own good. Think of what you can do for others.
1 CORINTHIANS 10:24

"Then a man from the country of Samaria came by. He went up to the [injured] man. As he saw him, he had loving-pity on him."
LUKE 10:33

"You must have loving-kindness just as your Father has loving-kindness."
LUKE 6:36

Be happy with those who are happy. Be sad with those who are sad.
ROMANS 12:15

Lord, touch my heart!
Make me compassionate.
I want to care more, Father!

. . . .

Lord, please show me how to be compassionate just like You. I want to care—really care—about people around me who are hurting. Show me how to love the ones who get made fun of or bullied. It's not always easy. Sometimes I go along with the crowd, but that's not a good idea. I want to help protect people and that starts with caring. Show me how to help those who feel like they don't fit in. I want to be more like You, Father—gracious and filled with compassion for those who are lonely and left out. Give me Your heart, I pray. Amen.

CONSEQUENCES

Every action has an equal and opposite reaction. That's what you learned in Science class.

When you push a swing in one direction, it swings back in the other direction. When you add ice to a glass of water, the water rises. Things change when action takes place.

The same is true when people bully other people. It hurts the person being bullied, of course, but it always comes back to hurt the bully as well. Think about the last time *you* hurt or offended someone on purpose. Didn't you start to feel guilty after a while? Didn't you wish you could go back and undo your words or actions?

Let's guard the things we say and do so that our actions don't have difficult consequences.

"All these good things will come upon you if you will obey the Lord your God."
DEUTERONOMY 28:2

"Good will come to you in the city, and good will come to you in the country. Good will come to your children, and the fruit of your ground, and the young of your animals. Your cattle and flock will have many young ones. Good will come to your basket and your bread pan. Good will come to you when you come in, and when you go out."
DEUTERONOMY 28:3–6

Bring up a child by teaching him the way he should go, and when he is old he will not turn away from it.
PROVERBS 22:6

There is no joy while we are being punished. It is hard to take, but later we can see that good came from it. And it gives us the peace of being right with God.
HEBREWS 12:11

You get what is coming to you when you sin. It is death! But God's free gift is life that lasts forever. It is given to us by our Lord Jesus Christ.
ROMANS 6:23

"The heart is fooled more than anything else, and is very sinful. Who can know how bad it is? I the Lord look into the heart, and test the mind. I give to each man what he should have because of his ways and because of the fruit that comes from his works."
JEREMIAH 17:9–10

The Lord is not slow about keeping His promise as some people think. He is waiting for you. The Lord does not want any person to be punished forever. He wants all people to be sorry for their sins and turn from them.
2 PETER 3:9

Leaders are God's servants to help you. If you do wrong, you should be afraid. They have the power to punish you. They work for God. They do what God wants done to those who do wrong.
ROMANS 13:4

A sinful man is trapped by his sins, but a man who is right with God sings for joy.
PROVERBS 29:6

The stick and strong words give wisdom, but a child who gets his own way brings shame to his mother.
PROVERBS 29:15

But your wrong-doings have kept you away from your God. Your sins have hidden His face from you, so that He does not hear.
ISAIAH 59:2

Anyone who does not take care of his family and those in his house has turned away from the faith. He is worse than a person who has never put his trust in Christ.
1 TIMOTHY 5:8

Honor will be given to the wise, but shame will be given to fools.
PROVERBS 3:35

A man who does what is right but gives way in front of the sinful, is like a well of mud or poisoned water.
PROVERBS 25:26

David was very angry at the man, and said to Nathan, "As the Lord lives, for sure the man who has done this should die. And he must pay four times the worth of the lamb, because he did this thing without pity."
2 SAMUEL 12:5–6

Then Judas was sorry he had handed Jesus over when he saw that Jesus was going to be killed. He took back the thirty pieces of silver and gave it to the head religious leaders and the other leaders. He said, "I have sinned because I handed over a Man Who has done no wrong." And they said, "What is that to us? That is your own doing."
MATTHEW 27:3–4

A man who is right with God hates lies, but the actions of a sinful man are hated and he is put to shame.
PROVERBS 13:5

"Those who are wise will shine like the bright heavens. And those who lead many to do what is right and good will shine like the stars forever and ever."
DANIEL 12:3

Do you not know that your body is a house of God where the Holy Spirit lives? God gave you His Holy Spirit. Now you belong to God. You do not belong to yourselves. God bought you with a great price. So honor God with your body. You belong to Him.
1 CORINTHIANS 6:19–20

"These will go to the place where they will be punished forever. But those right with God will have life that lasts forever."
MATTHEW 25:46

What is right and good watches over the one whose way is without blame, but sin destroys the sinful.
PROVERBS 13:6

Jesus said to him, "Put your sword back where it belongs. Everyone who uses a sword will die with a sword."
MATTHEW 26:52

Whatever your hand finds to do, do it with all your strength. For there is no work or planning or learning or wisdom in the place of the dead where you are going.
ECCLESIASTES 9:10

For all men have sinned and have missed the shining-greatness of God.
ROMANS 3:23

A sinful man is trapped by the sin of his lips, but those who are right with God will get away from trouble.
PROVERBS 12:13

His own sins will trap the sinful. He will be held with the ropes of his sin.
PROVERBS 5:22

This is what happened: Sin came into the world by one man, Adam. Sin brought death with it. Death spread to all men because all have sinned.
ROMANS 5:12

Fathers, do not be too hard on your children so they will become angry. Teach them in their growing years with Christian teaching.
EPHESIANS 6:4

I don't like consequences, Lord!
I wish my actions didn't always have reactions.
Sometimes I wish I could go back and change
the things I've said and done. . . .
Can I? Please?

. . . .

Lord, sometimes I've learned hard lessons. I've
mistreated others and regretted it later. I've lied to
my teacher and then got caught. There was a price
to pay. I don't want to have to pay a price. I want
to do the right thing the first time around. Can you
show me how, in the moment? When I'm tempted to
join the crowd or hurt someone's feelings because
they look or act different, help me to stop, think,
and respond the way You would respond, Lord.
If I act like You, there won't be a price to pay.

DOUBT

You want to believe things can change. You want to have faith that God will give you good friends who won't make fun of you or bully you. But sometimes you doubt.

People hurt your feelings, and that messes with your head and heart. You want to give up, crawl into a hole, and hide from the world. You want to be left alone.

But God doesn't want you to give up. He longs for you to be confident, to have faith that things will get better. He's on your side, you know. God is your defender, your friend, and the one who knows and loves you best.

You can trust Him. Don't doubt. Keep your head up. Better days are coming.

You must have faith as you ask [the Lord]. You must not doubt.
JAMES 1:6

Jesus said to them, "For sure, I tell you this: If you have faith and do not doubt, you will. . .be able to say to this mountain, 'Move from here and be thrown into the sea,' and it will be done."
MATTHEW 21:21

"For sure, I tell you, a person may say to this mountain, 'Move from here into the sea.' And if he does not doubt, but believes that what he says will be done, it will happen."
MARK 11:23

At once Jesus put out His hand and took hold of him. Jesus said to Peter, "You have so little faith! Why did you doubt?"
MATTHEW 14:31

Have loving-kindness for those who doubt.
JUDE 22

The man who has two ways of thinking changes in everything he does.
JAMES 1:8

At once the father cried out. He said with tears in his eyes, "Lord, I have faith. Help my weak faith to be stronger!"
MARK 9:24

"Do not fear, for I am with you. Do not be afraid, for I am your God. I will give you strength, and for sure I will help you. Yes, I will hold you up with My right hand that is right and good."
ISAIAH 41:10

Jesus said to them, "Why are you afraid? Why do you have doubts in your hearts?"
LUKE 24:38

Anyone who doubts is like a wave which is pushed around by the sea.
JAMES 1:6

[Jesus] said to Thomas, "Put your finger into My hands. Put your hand into My side. Do not doubt, believe!"
JOHN 20:27

But if he has doubts about the food he eats, God says he is guilty when he eats it. It is because he is eating without faith. Anything that is not done in faith is sin.
ROMANS 14:23

Now faith is being sure we will get what we hope for. It is being sure of what we cannot see.
HEBREWS 11:1

Because Noah had faith, he built a large boat for his family. God told him what was going to happen. His faith made him hear God speak and he obeyed. His family was saved from death because he built the boat.
HEBREWS 11:7A

In this way, Noah showed the world how sinful it was. Noah became right with God because of his faith in God.
HEBREWS 11:7B

Jesus said to them, "Have faith in God."
MARK 11:22

Zacharias said to the angel, "How can I know this for sure? I am old and my wife is old also." The angel said to him, "My name is Gabriel. I stand near God. He sent me to talk to you and bring to you this good news. See! You will not be able to talk until the day this happens. It is because you did not believe my words. What I said will happen at the right time."
LUKE 1:18–20

A man cannot please God unless he has faith. Anyone who comes to God must believe that He is. That one must also know that God gives what is promised to the one who keeps on looking for Him.
HEBREWS 11:6

For God did not give us a spirit of fear. He gave us a spirit of power and of love and of a good mind.
2 TIMOTHY 1:7

Abram believed in the Lord, and that made him right with God.
GENESIS 15:6

Our life is lived by faith. We do not live by what we see in front of us.
2 CORINTHIANS 5:7

Jesus said to him, "Thomas, because you have seen Me, you believe. Those are happy who have never seen Me and yet believe!"
JOHN 20:29

When they saw Jesus, they worshiped Him. But some did not believe.
MATTHEW 28:17

In my fear I said, "You have closed Your eyes to me!" But You heard my cry for loving-kindness when I called to You.
PSALM 31:22

I would have been without hope if I had not believed that I would see the loving-kindness of the Lord in the land of the living.
PSALM 27:13

"Do not let your heart be troubled. You have put your trust in God, put your trust in Me also."
JOHN 14:1

All this helps us know that what the early preachers said was true. You will do well to listen to what they have said. Their words are as lights that shine in a dark place. Listen until you understand what they have said. Then it will be like the morning light which takes away the darkness. And the Morning Star (Christ) will rise to shine in your hearts.
2 PETER 1:19

But the wisdom that comes from heaven is first of all pure. Then it gives peace. It is gentle and willing to obey. It is full of loving-kindness and of doing good. It has no doubts and does not pretend to be something it is not.
JAMES 3:17

Abraham did not doubt God's promise. His faith in God was strong, and he gave thanks to God.
ROMANS 4:20

We believe that Jesus died and then came to life again. Because we believe this, we know that God will bring to life again all those who belong to Jesus.
1 THESSALONIANS 4:14

One minute I believe, the next minute I doubt.
One minute I'm sure You'll come through for me, God.
The next minute I'm scared all over again.

• •

It's not always easy to keep the faith, Lord.
Sometimes I doubt Your goodness. I don't know
if You're really my defender and my friend. I wonder
if anyone's on my side at all. Will You desert me like
others have? Will You turn Your back on me? No—
You've promised that You will stick with me, no matter
what. Even if I mess up, You're right there. I never
have to doubt as long as I place my trust in You.
Thank You for that reminder, Father!

eNemies

Have you ever felt surrounded by enemies? Are there people in your world who keep irritating and upsetting you? How do you escape people like that? If you're like most kids, you have enemies. Of course, it was never your plan to have them. In fact, you wish you had friends, friends, and more friends. But somehow enemies keep showing up. How do you deal with them? That's a good question.

The Bible says that you are to love your enemies and to treat them the way you want to be treated. That's not easy, is it? But it's God's plan. Who's annoying you today? Take some time—right now—to pray for them. Go on! Do it! Then watch what God does as you forgive those who've hurt you.

"I say to you who hear Me, love those who work against you. Do good to those who hate you."
LUKE 6:27

Pray and give thanks for those who make trouble for you. Yes, pray for them instead of talking against them.
ROMANS 12:14

Do not be full of joy when the one who hates you falls. Do not let your heart be glad when he trips.
PROVERBS 24:17

"Be strong and have strength of heart. Do not be afraid or shake with fear because of them. For the Lord your God is the One Who goes with you. He will be faithful to you. He will not leave you alone."
DEUTERONOMY 31:6

"If you love those who love you, what pay can you expect from that? Sinners also love those who love them. If you do good to those who do good to you, what pay can you expect from that? Sinners also do good to those who do good to them."
LUKE 6:32–33

"If the one who hates you is hungry, feed him. If he is thirsty, give him water. If you do that, you will be making him more ashamed of himself."
ROMANS 12:20

"You have heard that it has been said, 'You must love your neighbor and hate those who hate you.' But I tell you, love those who hate you. (Respect and give thanks for those who say bad things to you. Do good to those who hate you.) Pray for those who do bad things to you and who make it hard for you."
MATTHEW 5:43–44

"His sun shines on bad people and on good people. He sends rain on those who are right with God and on those who are not right with God. If you love those who love you, what reward can you expect from that? Do not even the tax-gatherers do that? If you say hello only to the people you like, are you doing any more than others? The people who do not know God do that much."
MATTHEW 5:45–47

Even if I walk into trouble, You [Lord] will keep my life safe. You will put out Your hand against the anger of those who hate me. And Your right hand will save me.
PSALM 138:7

When the ways of a man are pleasing to the Lord, He makes even those who hate him to be at peace with him.

PROVERBS 16:7

Then Jesus said, "Father, forgive them. They do not know what they are doing." And they divided His clothes by drawing names.

LUKE 23:34

Do not trouble yourself because of sinful men. Do not want to be like those who do wrong. For they will soon dry up like the grass. Like the green plant they will soon die. Trust in the Lord, and do good. So you will live in the land and will be fed. Be happy in the Lord. And He will give you the desires of your heart. Give your way over to the Lord. Trust in Him also. And He will do it.

PSALM 37:1–5

The people of Israel did not remember the Lord their God, Who had saved them from the power of all those around who hated them.

JUDGES 8:34

If the one who hates you is hungry, feed him. If he is thirsty, give him water. If you do that, you will be making him more ashamed of himself, and the Lord will reward you.

PROVERBS 25:21–22

But if you obey [the angel's] voice and do all that I say, then I [the Lord] will hate those who hate you and fight against those who fight against you.

EXODUS 23:22

Be pleased to save me, O Lord. Hurry, O Lord, to help me. Let all who want to destroy my life be ashamed and troubled. Let those who want to hurt me be turned away without honor. Let those who say to me, "O! O!" be filled with fear because of their shame.

PSALM 40:13–15

Yes, even if I walk through the valley of the shadow of death, I will not be afraid of anything, because You are with me. You have a walking stick with which to guide and one with which to help. These comfort me.

PSALM 23:4

You [Lord] are making a table of food ready for me in front of those who hate me. You have poured oil on my head. I have everything I need.
PSALM 23:5

Keep me safe, Lord, and set me free. Do not let me be put to shame for I put my trust in You.
PSALM 25:20

"The Lord will fight for you. All you have to do is keep still."
EXODUS 14:14

"God told us that we should be saved from those who hate us and from all those who work against us."
LUKE 1:71

"If you see the donkey of one who hates you falling under its load, do not leave the problem to him. Help him to free the animal."
EXODUS 23:5

O Lord, lead me in what is right and good, because of the ones who hate me. Make Your way straight in front of me.
PSALM 5:8

"You have heard that it has been said, 'An eye for an eye and a tooth for a tooth.' But I tell you, do not fight with the man who wants to fight. Whoever hits you on the right side of the face, turn so he can hit the other side also."
MATTHEW 5:38–39

We work with our hands to make a living. We speak kind words to those who speak against us. When people hurt us, we say nothing.
1 CORINTHIANS 4:12

"See, I [the Lord your God] am sending an angel before you to keep you safe on the way. He will bring you to the place I have made ready."
EXODUS 23:20

He who lives in the safe place of the Most High will be in the shadow of the All-powerful.
PSALM 91:1

[The Lord] will cover you with His wings. And under His wings you will be safe. He is faithful like a safe-covering and a strong wall.
PSALM 91:4

Help! I'm surrounded!
My enemies are swallowing me alive!
Why won't they leave me alone, Lord?
What did I ever do to deserve this?

· ·

Lord, I know that You will protect me from my enemies, so today I'm asking You to do that. Keep me safe, I pray. And Lord, show me how to forgive those who've hurt me. You're a miracle-working God. You can take enemies and turn them into friends in no time. In the meantime, show me how to make things better, not worse. I won't get angry. I won't get even. Instead, I'll show grace and mercy. . .while I keep my distance! I'm so grateful You've got my back, Lord.

FeAR

Are your knees knocking? Is your voice quivering? Are you scared that things will get worse before they get better?

No one likes to be afraid. It's bad enough to be scared of the dark but it's even worse to be afraid of people. Are there bullies at school or in your neighborhood who make you afraid? It's time to turn that fear into something positive.

The Bible says there is no fear in love because perfect love puts fear out of our hearts (see 1 John 4:18). When we love the way Christ loves, there's not much room left over for fear. Today, speak to your fears in the name of Jesus, and use God's perfect love to reach out to others.

There is no fear in love. Perfect love puts fear out of our hearts. People have fear when they are afraid of being punished. The man who is afraid does not have perfect love.

1 John 4:18

"Do not fear, for I am with you. Do not be afraid, for I am your God. I will give you strength, and for sure I will help you. Yes, I will hold you up with My right hand that is right and good."

Isaiah 41:10

For God did not give us a spirit of fear. He gave us a spirit of power and of love and of a good mind.

2 Timothy 1:7

I looked for the Lord, and He answered me. And He took away all my fears.

Psalm 34:4

And so my heart is glad. My soul is full of joy. My body also will rest without fear.

Psalm 16:9

The fear of man brings a trap, but he who trusts in the Lord will be honored.
PROVERBS 29:25

"Have I not told you? Be strong and have strength of heart! Do not be afraid or lose faith. For the Lord your God is with you anywhere you go."
JOSHUA 1:9

Do not worry. Learn to pray about everything. Give thanks to God as you ask Him for what you need.
PHILIPPIANS 4:6

When I am afraid, I will trust in You. I praise the Word of God. I have put my trust in God. I will not be afraid. What can only a man do to me?
PSALM 56:3–4

You should not act like people who are owned by someone. They are always afraid. Instead, the Holy Spirit makes us His sons, and we can call to Him, "My Father."
ROMANS 8:15

"Be strong and have strength of heart. Do not be afraid or shake with fear because of them. For the Lord your God is the One Who goes with you. He will be faithful to you. He will not leave you alone."
DEUTERONOMY 31:6

The Lord is my light and the One Who saves me. Whom should I fear? The Lord is the strength of my life. Of whom should I be afraid?
PSALM 27:1

For I know that nothing can keep us from the love of God. Death cannot! Life cannot! Angels cannot! Leaders cannot! Any other power cannot! Hard things now or in the future cannot! The world above or the world below cannot! Any other living thing cannot keep us away from the love of God which is ours through Christ Jesus our Lord.
ROMANS 8:38–39

"Peace I [the Lord] leave with you. My peace I give to you. I do not give peace to you as the world gives. Do not let your hearts be troubled or afraid."
JOHN 14:27

But now the Lord Who made you, O Jacob, and He Who made you, O Israel, says, "Do not be afraid. For I have bought you and made you free. I have called you by name. You are Mine!"
ISAIAH 43:1

The fear of the Lord leads to life, and he who has it will sleep well, and will not be touched by sin.
PROVERBS 19:23

The fear of the Lord is the beginning of wisdom. All who obey His Laws have good understanding. His praise lasts forever.
PSALM 111:10

Give all your worries to [Christ] because He cares for you.
1 PETER 5:7

"Do not be afraid of them who kill the body. They are not able to kill the soul. But fear [the Lord] Who is able to destroy both soul and body in hell."
MATTHEW 10:28

He preached without fear in the name of the Lord.
ACTS 9:29

The Lord is with me. I will not be afraid of what man can do to me.
PSALM 118:6

Do not worry. Learn to pray about everything. Give thanks to God as you ask Him for what you need. The peace of God is much greater than the human mind can understand. This peace will keep your hearts and minds through Christ Jesus.
PHILIPPIANS 4:6–7

Jesus said to His followers, "Because of this, I say to you, do not worry about your life, what you are going to eat. Do not worry about your body, what you are going to wear. Life is worth more than food. The body is worth more than clothes."
LUKE 12:22–23

The fear of the Lord is to hate what is sinful. I hate pride, self-love, the way of sin, and lies.
PROVERBS 8:13

"You will not be afraid of them. For the Lord your God is among you, a great and powerful God."
DEUTERONOMY 7:21

The fear of the Lord is a well of life. Its waters keep a man from death.
PROVERBS 14:27

"For I am the Lord your God Who holds your right hand, and Who says to you, 'Do not be afraid. I will help you.'"
ISAIAH 41:13

Paul saw the Lord in a dream one night. He said to Paul, "Do not be afraid. Keep speaking. Do not close your mouth. I am with you. No one will hurt you. I have many people in this city who belong to Me."
ACTS 18:9–10

When I am afraid, I will trust in You [God].
PSALM 56:3

Fear, be gone in Jesus' name!
You have no place in my heart or my mind.

....

Lord, today I come to You with all of my fears.
Sometimes I feel afraid of being alone. Other
times I'm scared of what bullies will say or do to
hurt my feelings. Sometimes I'm just scared for no
reason at all. It's like fear is a tight sweater and it's
making me uncomfortable. Today I give my fears to
You, Father. You can take them and replace them
with peace. Show me how to look fear in the face
and say, "Be gone, in Jesus' name!"

FORGIVENESS

You know she's up to no good. You watched her do it: she lied to the teacher and got away with it.

There are times when it seems like the bad guys win and the good guys lose. What's up with that?

Even though it's hard to do, Jesus wants you to forgive people who have wronged you or other people you care about. Why? Because that's what He does for everyone who believes in Jesus.

Does that mean you keep putting up with their bullying? No way! You have to let an adult know right away if someone is being hurt. But you can still forgive the one who did the bullying.

Forgiveness is like a key that unlocks a prison door. You hold the key in your hand. Will you use it?

"When you stand to pray, if you have anything against anyone, forgive him. Then your Father in heaven will forgive your sins also."
MARK 11:25

"If you do not forgive people their sins, your Father will not forgive your sins."
MATTHEW 6:15

Then Peter came to Jesus and said, "Lord, how many times may my brother sin against me and I forgive him, up to seven times?" Jesus said to him, "I tell you, not seven times but seventy times seven!"
MATTHEW 18:21–22

"Do not say what is wrong in other people's lives. Then other people will not say what is wrong in your life. Do not say someone is guilty. Then other people will not say you are guilty. Forgive other people and other people will forgive you."
LUKE 6:37

Love takes everything that comes without giving up.
1 CORINTHIANS 13:7

Try to understand other people. Forgive each other. If you have something against someone, forgive him. That is the way the Lord forgave you.
COLOSSIANS 3:13

Tell your sins to each other. And pray for each other so you may be healed. The prayer from the heart of a man right with God has much power.
JAMES 5:16

Who can see his own mistakes? Forgive my sins that I do not see.
PSALM 19:12

My sins are strong against me. But You [God] forgive our sins.
PSALM 65:3

Dear friend, do not follow what is sinful, but follow what is good. The person who does what is good belongs to God.
3 JOHN 11

For all men have sinned and have missed the shining-greatness of God.
ROMANS 3:23

He has taken our sins from us as far as the east is from the west. The Lord has loving-pity on those who fear Him, as a father has loving-pity on his children. For He knows what we are made of. He remembers that we are dust.
PSALM 103:12–14

Hate starts fights, but love covers all sins.
PROVERBS 10:12

Peter said to them, "Be sorry for your sins and turn from them and be baptized in the name of Jesus Christ, and your sins will be forgiven. You will receive the gift of the Holy Spirit."
ACTS 2:38

"Forgive us our sins as we forgive those who sin against us."
MATTHEW 6:12

"If you forgive people their sins, your Father in heaven will forgive your sins also."
MATTHEW 6:14

You have never been tempted to sin in any different way than other people. God is faithful. He will not allow you to be tempted more than you can take. But when you are tempted, He will make a way for you to keep from falling into sin.

1 CORINTHIANS 10:13

Because of the blood of Christ, we are bought and made free from the punishment of sin. And because of His blood, our sins are forgiven. His loving-favor to us is so rich.

EPHESIANS 1:7

"Watch yourselves! If your brother sins, speak sharp words to him. If he is sorry and turns from his sin, forgive him. What if he sins against you seven times in one day? If he comes to you and says he is sorry and turns from his sin, forgive him."

LUKE 17:3–4

He who covers a sin looks for love. He who tells of trouble separates good friends.

PROVERBS 17:9

"Come now, let us think about this together," says the Lord. "Even though your sins are bright red, they will be as white as snow. Even though they are dark red, they will be like wool."
Isaiah 1:18

"But you must be sorry for your sins and turn from them."
Acts 3:19a

It will not go well for the man who hides his sins, but he who tells his sins and turns from them will be given loving-pity.
Proverbs 28:13

Then Jesus said, "Father, forgive them. They do not know what they are doing." And they divided His clothes by drawing names.
Luke 23:34

"O Lord our God, You are kind and forgiving, even when we would not obey You."
Daniel 9:9

"This is My blood of the New Way of Worship which is given for many. It is given so the sins of many can be forgiven."
MATTHEW 26:28

I told my sin to You. I did not hide my wrong-doing. I said, "I will tell my sins to the Lord." And You forgave the guilt of my sin.
PSALM 32:5

"You must turn to God and have your sins taken away. Then many times your soul will receive new strength from the Lord."
ACTS 3:19B

For sure there is not a right and good man on earth who always does good and never sins.
ECCLESIASTES 7:20

"For God so loved the world that He gave His only Son. Whoever puts his trust in God's Son will not be lost but will have life that lasts forever."
JOHN 3:16

Lord, I'm holding the key in my hand right now.
My fingers are squeezing it tight!
I want to use it for good.
I want to forgive. . .but can I?

· ·

Father, help me to forgive the ones who have hurt my feelings or who've been rude to my friends. It's so hard. Sometimes it seems impossible. But You've forgiven me, Lord, and with Your help I can truly forgive others. When I use my key of forgiveness to unlock that door, then bullies can be set free from the prison they are in. Their hearts can be turned around for good. Help me to use my key, Lord.

FRIENDS

First he acts like he's your friend, then he turns on you! Is he going to stick by you, or what?

It's hard to know who to trust. Some people claim to be your friend, but then you find out they're talking about you behind your back or saying mean things.

God wants you to have amazing friendships. There are lots of kids out there longing for a good friend like you. So keep your eyes and ears wide open for new possibilities. That kid who sits alone at lunch? He wants to be your friend. That girl who doesn't seem to fit in? You could bring a smile to her face by including her.

Today, be the kind of friend that Jesus has been to you.

A man who has friends must be a friend, but there is a friend who stays nearer than a brother.
PROVERBS 18:24

Two are better than one, because they have good pay for their work. For if one of them falls, the other can help him up. But it is hard for the one who falls when there is no one to lift him up. And if two lie down together, they keep warm. But how can one be warm alone? One man is able to have power over him who is alone, but two can stand against him. It is not easy to break a rope made of three strings.
ECCLESIASTES 4:9–12

"No one can have greater love than to give his life for his friends."
JOHN 15:13

Iron is made sharp with iron, and one man is made sharp by a friend.
PROVERBS 27:17

A friend loves at all times. A brother is born to share troubles.
PROVERBS 17:17

So comfort each other and make each other strong as you are already doing.
1 Thessalonians 5:11

I am a friend to all who fear You [God] and of those who keep Your Law.
Psalm 119:63

Oil and perfume make the heart glad, so are a man's words sweet to his friend.
Proverbs 27:9

The pains given by a friend are faithful, but the kisses of one who hates you are false.
Proverbs 27:6

"Kindness from a friend should be shown to a man without hope, or he might turn away from the fear of the All-powerful."
Job 6:14

A bad man spreads trouble. One who hurts people with bad talk separates good friends.
Proverbs 16:28

Let us help each other to love others and to do good. Let us not stay away from church meetings. Some people are doing this all the time. Comfort each other as you see the day of [Christ's] return coming near.
HEBREWS 10:24–25

Most of all, have a true love for each other. Love covers many sins. Be happy to have people stay for the night and eat with you. God has given each of you a gift. Use it to help each other. This will show God's loving-favor.
1 PETER 4:8–10

O Lord, who may live in Your tent? . . . He does not hurt others with his tongue, or do wrong to his neighbor, or bring shame to his friend.
PSALM 15:1, 3

You know how Timothy proved to be such a true friend to me [Paul] when we preached the Good News. He was like a son helping his father.
PHILIPPIANS 2:22

He who walks with wise men will be wise, but the one who walks with fools will be destroyed.
PROVERBS 13:20

Both of us need help. I can help make your faith strong and you can do the same for me. We need each other.
ROMANS 1:12

"This is what I tell you to do: Love each other just as I [the Lord] have loved you. No one can have greater love than to give his life for his friends. You are My friends if you do what I tell you."
JOHN 15:12–14

Do not have anything to do with a man given to anger, or go with a man who has a bad temper. Or you might learn his ways and get yourself into a trap.
PROVERBS 22:24–25

Do not be among those who make promises and put themselves up as trust for what others owe. If you have nothing with which to pay, why should he take your bed from under you?
PROVERBS 22:26–27

"Do for other people what you would like to have them do for you."
LUKE 6:31

And now we have these three: faith and hope and love, but the greatest of these is love.
1 CORINTHIANS 13:13

Sharp words spoken in the open are better than love that is hidden.
PROVERBS 27:5

The man who is right with God is a teacher to his neighbor, but the way of the sinful leads them the wrong way.
PROVERBS 12:26

It happened as the Holy Writings said it would happen. They say, "Abraham put his trust in God and he became right with God." He was called the friend of God.
JAMES 2:23

The one who is careful what he says will have good come to him, but the one who wants to hurt others will have trouble.

PROVERBS 13:2

Dear friends, let us love each other, because love comes from God. Those who love are God's children and they know God.

1 JOHN 4:7

He who stays away from others cares only about himself. He argues against all good wisdom.

PROVERBS 18:1

Do not leave your own friend or your father's friend alone.

PROVERBS 27:10

Keep your lives free from the love of money. Be happy with what you have. God has said, "I will never leave you or let you be alone."

HEBREWS 13:5

Lord, I get so confused!
It's so hard to know who to trust.
Are the people who say they're my
friends really my friends?

. . . .

God, please help me figure out which friends are safe
to hang out with. I need (and want) good friends,
but I want them to be true friends, the kind who will
stick with me, even when I'm down. Point me in the
direction of true, godly friends, Lord. And while You're
at it, please show me how I can be a better friend to
people around me, especially those who are being
bullied. I don't want to waste one minute. I want to be
the very best friend I can be. With Your help, I can!

THE GOLDEN RULE

Do unto others. . . *Before* they do unto you? *After* they do unto you? No, *as you wish* they would do unto you!

People just love to get even, don't they? It's human nature. Someone does something mean to you, and you want to do something mean to them. Someone talks bad about you, and you want to talk bad about them.

Jesus has a different way of dealing with mean people. He wants you to treat them the way you wish they had treated you, not the way they're actually treating you.

Ouch! That's hard! It means you've got to be nice, even when they're not. You've got to respond kindly, even when they don't. It's going to take patience, but with God's help, you can do it!

"Do for other people whatever you would like to have them do for you. This is what the Jewish Law and the early preachers said."
Matthew 7:12

"For God so loved the world that He gave His only Son. Whoever puts his trust in God's Son will not be lost but will have life that lasts forever."
John 3:16

"Do for other people what you would like to have them do for you."
Luke 6:31

You obey the whole Law when you do this one thing, "Love your neighbor as you love yourself."
Galatians 5:14

"Do not hurt someone who has hurt you. Do not keep on hating the sons of your people, but love your neighbor as yourself. I am the Lord."
Leviticus 19:18

You do well when you obey the Holy Writings which say, "You must love your neighbor as you love yourself."
James 2:8

When someone does something bad to you, do not do the same thing to him. When someone talks about you, do not talk about him. Instead, pray that good will come to him. You were called to do this so you might receive good things from God.
1 PETER 3:9

"Do not say what is wrong in other people's lives. Then other people will not say what is wrong in your life. You will be guilty of the same things you find in others. When you say what is wrong in others, your words will be used to say what is wrong in you."
MATTHEW 7:1–2

"Why do you look at the small piece of wood in your brother's eye, and do not see the big piece of wood in your own eye? How can you say to your brother, 'Let me take that small piece of wood out of your eye,' when there is a big piece of wood in your own eye? You who pretend to be someone you are not, first take the big piece of wood out of your own eye. Then you can see better to take the small piece of wood out of your brother's eye."
MATTHEW 7:3–5

"You have heard that it has been said, 'You must love your neighbor and hate those who hate you.' But I tell you, love those who hate you. (Respect and give thanks for those who say bad things to you. Do good to those who hate you.) Pray for those who do bad things to you and who make it hard for you."
MATTHEW 5:43–44

Do not owe anyone anything, but love each other. Whoever loves his neighbor has done what the Law says to do.
ROMANS 13:8

A man stood up who knew the Law and tried to trap Jesus. He said, "Teacher, what must I do to have life that lasts forever?" Jesus said to him, "What is written in the Law? What does the Law say?" The man said, "You must love the Lord your God with all your heart. You must love Him with all your soul. You must love Him with all your strength. You must love Him with all your mind. You must love your neighbor as you love yourself." Jesus said to him, "You have said the right thing. Do this and you will have life."
LUKE 10:25–28

"You must not steal. You must not tell a lie about another person. You must not want something someone else has." The Law also says that these and many other Laws are brought together in one Law, "You must love your neighbor as yourself." Anyone who loves his neighbor will do no wrong to him. You keep the Law with love.

ROMANS 13:9–10

Christian brothers, do not talk against anyone or speak bad things about each other. If a person says bad things about his brother, he is speaking against him. And he will be speaking against God's Law. If you say the Law is wrong, and do not obey it, you are saying you are better than the Law.

JAMES 4:11

"Those who show loving-kindness are happy, because they will have loving-kindness shown to them."

MATTHEW 5:7

"If you want joy in your life and have happy days, keep your tongue from saying bad things and your lips from talking bad about others."

1 PETER 3:10

If a person says, "I love God," but hates his brother, he is a liar. If a person does not love his brother whom he has seen, how can he love God Whom he has not seen?
1 JOHN 4:20

Put out of your life all these things: bad feelings about other people, anger, temper, loud talk, bad talk which hurts other people, and bad feelings which hurt other people. You must be kind to each other. Think of the other person. Forgive other people just as God forgave you because of Christ's death on the cross.
EPHESIANS 4:31–32

My Christian brothers, you know everyone should listen much and speak little. He should be slow to become angry. A man's anger does not allow him to be right with God.
JAMES 1:19–20

"No one can have greater love than to give his life for his friends."
JOHN 15:13

Then the teacher of the Law said, "Teacher, You have told the truth. There is one God. There is no other God but Him. A man should love Him with all his heart and with all his understanding. He should love Him with all his soul and with all his strength and love his neighbor as himself. This is more important than to bring animals to be burned on the altar or to give God other gifts on the altar in worship."
MARK 12:32–33

"What man among you would give his son a stone if he should ask for bread? Or if he asks for a fish, would he give him a snake? You are bad and you know how to give good things to your children. How much more will your Father in heaven give good things to those who ask Him?"
MATTHEW 7:9–11

"You must be perfect as your Father in heaven is perfect."
MATTHEW 5:48

"Then you may be the sons of your Father Who is in heaven. His sun shines on bad people and on good people. He sends rain on those who are right with God and on those who are not right with God."
MATTHEW 5:45

I'll do unto others, Lord!
I'll love, even when they don't love.
I'll serve, even when they don't serve.
I'll treat them nicely, even when they're mean to me.

....

I get it, Lord! You don't want me to get even with the bullies and meanies. You want me to treat them the way I want to be treated. I wanted to be treated kindly, so that means I have to step up my game and be kind to them, even when they're rude. I'll admit, that's not going to be easy. I'd rather give them a piece of my mind. But You're showing me a better way and I'm going to follow You.

HATE

"I hate broccoli!" "I hate wearing these old tennis shoes." "I hate doing my homework!"

How many times a day do you use the word *hate*? Probably a lot, right?

It's easy to talk about the things you hate, but when it comes to people, *hate* is a word God doesn't want you to use.

Oh sure, it's good to hate sin. And it's good to hate bullying. But the people committing the sins. . . the ones doing the bullying? God wants you to love them, not hate them. It's hard, for sure. But love is so much stronger than hate. It wins every time.

If a person says, "I love God," but hates his brother, he is a liar. If a person does not love his brother whom he has seen, how can he love God Whom he has not seen?
1 John 4:20

Hate starts fights, but love covers all sins.
Proverbs 10:12

A man who hates his brother is a killer in his heart. You know that life which lasts forever is not in one who kills.
1 John 3:15

There are six things which the Lord hates, yes, seven that are hated by Him: A proud look, a lying tongue, and hands that kill those who are without guilt, a heart that makes sinful plans, feet that run fast to sin, a person who tells lies about someone else, and one who starts fights among brothers.
Proverbs 6:16–19

"In your heart do not hate someone from your own country. You may speak sharp words to your neighbor, but do not sin because of him."
Leviticus 19:17

Whoever says he is in the light but hates his brother is still in darkness.
1 JOHN 2:9

Love does not give up. Love is kind. Love is not jealous. Love does not put itself up as being important. Love has no pride. Love does not do the wrong thing. Love never thinks of itself. Love does not get angry. Love does not remember the suffering that comes from being hurt by someone. Love is not happy with sin. Love is happy with the truth. Love takes everything that comes without giving up. Love believes all things. Love hopes for all things. Love keeps on in all things.
1 CORINTHIANS 13:4–7

Watch your talk! No bad words should be coming from your mouth. Say what is good. Your words should help others grow as Christians.
EPHESIANS 4:29

"If the world hates you, you know it hated Me [Jesus] before it hated you."
JOHN 15:18

A gentle answer turns away anger, but a sharp word causes anger.
PROVERBS 15:1

The fear of the Lord is to hate what is sinful. I hate pride, self-love, the way of sin, and lies.
PROVERBS 8:13

"I [Jesus] give you a new Law. You are to love each other. You must love each other as I have loved you. If you love each other, all men will know you are My followers."
JOHN 13:34–35

Let those who love the Lord hate what is bad. For He keeps safe the souls of His faithful ones. He takes them away from the hand of the sinful.
PSALM 97:10

"You will be hated by all people because of Me [Jesus]. But he who stays true to the end will be saved."
MATTHEW 10:22

"No one can have two bosses. He will hate the one and love the other. Or he will listen to the one and work against the other. You cannot have both God and riches as your boss at the same time."
MATTHEW 6:24

The Lord tests and proves those who are right and good and those who are sinful. And His soul hates the one who loves to hurt others.
PSALM 11:5

[Leaders] must not speak bad of anyone, and they must not argue. They should be gentle and kind to all people.
TITUS 3:2

If you are angry, do not let it become sin. Get over your anger before the day is finished.
EPHESIANS 4:26

A dish of vegetables with love is better than eating the best meat with hate.
PROVERBS 15:17

The proud cannot stand before You [Lord]. You hate all who do wrong.
PSALM 5:5

He who hides hate has lying lips, and he who talks to hurt people is a fool.
PROVERBS 10:18

Put out of your life all these things: bad feelings about other people, anger, temper, loud talk, bad talk which hurts other people, and bad feelings which hurt other people.
EPHESIANS 4:31

The things your sinful old self wants to do are: . . . hating, fighting, being jealous, being angry, arguing, dividing into little groups and thinking the other groups are wrong, false teaching, wanting something someone else has, killing other people, using strong drink, wild parties, and all things like these. I told you before and I am telling you again that those who do these things will have no place in the holy nation of God.
GALATIANS 5:19–21

I hate what is false, but I love Your Law.
PSALM 119:163

I hate the meeting of sinners, and will not sit with the sinful.
PSALM 26:5

He who hates covers it up with his lips, but stores up false ways in his heart. When he speaks with kindness, do not believe him, for there are seven things that are hated in his heart. Even if his hate is covered with false ways, his sin will be found out in front of the great meeting.
PROVERBS 26:24–26

Put away the old person you used to be. Have nothing to do with your old sinful life. It was sinful because of being fooled into following bad desires.
EPHESIANS 4:22

Anyone who loves his neighbor will do no wrong to him. You keep the Law with love.
ROMANS 13:10

I'm laying it down, Lord.
I won't pick it back up again!
Hate has to go, in Jesus' name!

• •

Lord, today I make a promise to stop hating.
I'll do my best to love even the hardest-to-love
people. (This is so tough, Lord!) But I've learned
one thing: When I hate them, my heart grows hard
and heavy. I don't like the way that feels. You're a
lover, not a hater, God, and I want to be more like
You. So today I lay my hatred down and will do
my best not to pick it back up again.

HeLP

Where can you go to find it? How come some people give it and others don't? What about you? Are you a helper?

When you're really in trouble, who do you go to? Your teacher? Your parents? A trusted neighbor? A friend? A preacher?

Sometimes it's hard to know where the helpers are. The truth is, some adults—even the best ones—get busy and distracted. They don't seem to notice when you're hurting.

That's why it's so good to know that God is your very best helper. No matter what you're facing today, you can turn to Him. He's there. . .and He cares.

This doesn't mean you should give up on your friends and the adults in your life. But they're just people too. God is the only perfect helper.

I will lift up my eyes to the mountains. Where will my help come from? My help comes from the Lord, Who made heaven and earth.

PSALM 121:1–2

"Do not fear, for I am with you. Do not be afraid, for I am your God. I will give you strength, and for sure I will help you. Yes, I will hold you up with My right hand that is right and good."

ISAIAH 41:10

Then they cried out to the Lord in their trouble. And He saved them from their suffering. He brought them out of darkness and the shadow of death. And He broke their chains.

PSALM 107:13–14

Do not throw away your trust, for your reward will be great.

HEBREWS 10:35

"Yes, if you ask anything in My [Jesus'] name, I will do it."

JOHN 14:14

See, God is my Helper. The Lord is the One Who keeps my soul alive.
PSALM 54:4

The Lord is with me. He is my Helper. I will watch those lose who fight against me.
PSALM 118:7

Give your way over to the Lord. Trust in Him also. And He will do it.
PSALM 37:5

"The Lord will fight for you. All you have to do is keep still."
EXODUS 14:14

Then Asa called to the Lord his God and said, "Lord, there is no one but You to help in the battle between the powerful and the weak. So help us, O Lord God. For we trust in You. In Your name we have come against these many people. O Lord, You are our God. Do not let any man win the fight against You."
2 CHRONICLES 14:11

Those who are right with the Lord cry, and He hears them. And He takes them from all their troubles.
PSALM 34:17

"Then I will ask My Father and He will give you another Helper. He will be with you forever."
JOHN 14:16

For [God] will take out of trouble the one in need when he cries for help, and the poor man who has no one to help.
PSALM 72:12

Because I suffer and am in need, let the Lord think of me. You are my help and the One Who sets me free. O my God, do not wait.
PSALM 40:17

So we can say for sure, "The Lord is my Helper. I am not afraid of anything man can do to me."
HEBREWS 13:6

My help comes from the Lord, Who made heaven and earth. He will not let your feet go out from under you. He Who watches over you will not sleep.
PSALM 121:2–3

"Do not let your heart be troubled. You have put your trust in God, put your trust in Me [Jesus] also."
JOHN 14:1

This poor man cried, and the Lord heard him. And He saved him out of all his troubles.
PSALM 34:6

Hear, O Lord. And show me loving-kindness. O Lord, be my Helper.
PSALM 30:10

The Lord is my strength and my safe cover. My heart trusts in Him, and I am helped. So my heart is full of joy. I will thank Him with my song.
PSALM 28:7

A man who does what is right and good may have many troubles. But the Lord takes him out of them all.
PSALM 34:19

"The Helper (Holy Spirit) will tell about Me when He comes. I will send Him to you from the Father. He is the Spirit of Truth and comes from the Father. You will also tell of Me because you have been with Me from the beginning."
JOHN 15:26–27

"The Helper is the Holy Spirit. The Father will send Him in My place. He will teach you everything and help you remember everything I have told you."
JOHN 14:26

Give your way over to the Lord. Trust in Him also. And He will do it. He will make your being right and good show as the light, and your wise actions as the noon day.
PSALM 37:5–6

God is our safe place and our strength. He is always our help when we are in trouble.
PSALM 46:1

The Lord also keeps safe those who suffer. He is a safe place in times of trouble.
PSALM 9:9

[God] sent His Word and healed them. And He saved them from the grave.
PSALM 107:20

Let the joy of Your saving power return to me. And give me a willing spirit to obey You [God].
PSALM 51:12

You pushed me back so that I was falling, but the Lord helped me.
PSALM 118:13

But You, O Lord, be not far from me! O my Strength, hurry to help me!
PSALM 22:19

Help!
I need You, Lord!
My friends and family members are distracted.
They don't seem to notice I'm hurting. . .but You do.

·····························

Lord, I'm so glad You're paying attention. You see me. You know what I'm going through. You know when my feelings are hurt by the mean kids or when I feel left out. You come rushing to my rescue. You dry my tears and whisper, "It's going to be okay" in my ear. Thank You for being the best helper of all, Lord. I want to be more like You so that I can help others who are being bullied or left out.

LONELINESS

Sometimes it happens in a crowd. Sometimes it happens when you're all alone in your room. Feeling lonely? Everyone goes through it. So why do you feel like you're the only one?

Most people struggle with loneliness, whether they talk about it or not. It's easy to feel like you're invisible, even when you're surrounded by people.

What can you do about that? Ask God to erase these feelings and replace them with His joy. Begin to reach out to others who look lonely.

Instead of focusing on yourself, do something special for someone else. When you shift your focus, loneliness fades away. It's time to tell loneliness to get lost!

Then the Lord God said, "It is not good for man to be alone. I will make a helper that is right for him."
GENESIS 2:18

"Do not fear, for I am with you. Do not be afraid, for I am your God. I will give you strength, and for sure I will help you. Yes, I will hold you up with My right hand that is right and good."
ISAIAH 41:10

"Be strong and have strength of heart. Do not be afraid or shake with fear because of them. For the Lord your God is the One Who goes with you. He will be faithful to you. He will not leave you alone."
DEUTERONOMY 31:6

Give all your worries to [God] because He cares for you.
1 PETER 5:7

"Teach them to do all the things I [Jesus] have told you. And I am with you always, even to the end of the world."
MATTHEW 28:20

For my father and my mother have left me. But the Lord will take care of me.
PSALM 27:10

Yes, even if I walk through the valley of the shadow of death, I will not be afraid of anything, because You [Lord] are with me. You have a walking stick with which to guide and one with which to help. These comfort me.
PSALM 23:4

"No man will be able to stand against you all the days of your life. I [God] will be with you just as I have been with Moses. I will be faithful to you and will not leave you alone."
JOSHUA 1:5

People make it hard for us, but we are not left alone. We are knocked down, but we are not destroyed.
2 CORINTHIANS 4:9

"I [Jesus] will not leave you without help as children without parents. I will come to you."
JOHN 14:18

Do not worry. Learn to pray about everything. Give thanks to God as you ask Him for what you need. The peace of God is much greater than the human mind can understand. This peace will keep your hearts and minds through Christ Jesus.

PHILIPPIANS 4:6–7

Keep on loving each other as Christian brothers. Do not forget to be kind to strangers and let them stay in your home. Some people have had angels in their homes without knowing it.

HEBREWS 13:1–2

Those who know Your name will put their trust in You. For You, O Lord, have never left alone those who look for You.

PSALM 9:10

Keep your lives free from the love of money. Be happy with what you have. God has said, "I will never leave you or let you be alone."

HEBREWS 13:5

God in His holy house is a father to those who have no father. And He keeps the women safe whose husbands have died. God makes a home for those who are alone. He leads men out of prison into happiness and well-being. But those who fight against Him live in an empty desert.
PSALM 68:5–6

He heals those who have a broken heart. He heals their sorrows.
PSALM 147:3

Trust in Him at all times, O people. Pour out your heart before Him. God is a safe place for us.
PSALM 62:8

A man who has friends must be a friend, but there is a friend who stays nearer than a brother.
PROVERBS 18:24

Turn to me and show me Your loving-kindness. For I am alone and in trouble.
PSALM 25:16

[God] gives strength to the weak. And He gives power to him who has little strength.
ISAIAH 40:29

[God] has given us His Spirit. This is how we live by His help and He lives in us.
1 JOHN 4:13

"The Lord is the One Who goes before you. He will be with you. He will be faithful to you and will not leave you alone. Do not be afraid or troubled."
DEUTERONOMY 31:8

"The time is coming, yes, it is already here when you will be going your own way. Everyone will go to his own house and leave Me [Jesus] alone. Yet I am not alone because the Father is with Me."
JOHN 16:32

But Ruth said, "Do not beg me to leave you or turn away from following you. I will go where you go. I will live where you live. Your people will be my people. And your God will be my God."
RUTH 1:16

"The Lord will not leave His people alone, because of His great name. The Lord has been pleased to make you His people."
1 SAMUEL 12:22

What can we say about all these things? Since God is for us, who can be against us?
ROMANS 8:31

I will lift up my eyes to the mountains. Where will my help come from? My help comes from the Lord, Who made heaven and earth.
PSALM 121:1–2

At my first trial no one helped me. Everyone left me. I hope this will not be held against them. But the Lord was with me. He gave me power to preach the Good News so all the people who do not know God might hear.
2 TIMOTHY 4:16–17

Lord, all my desire is before You. And my breathing deep within is not hidden from You.
PSALM 38:9

*This feeling in my heart. . .
It's hard to describe.
Sometimes it feels like a hole,
an empty space,
but I know You can fill it up, Lord.*

. . . .

*Lord, I don't like feeling alone. Sometimes it
happens when I'm in a crowd, especially if people
are deliberately leaving me out or making me feel
like I'm not good enough. The mean kids have worked
extra-hard to make me feel left out. I'm so glad You're
with me all the time, Lord. I'm never alone as long
as I'm with You. Show me who I can talk to today.
Someone else is feeling lonely too, and I want to
brighten their day. With Your help, I can.*

Love

Is it a feeling? Is it an action? What is love, anyway? Some people think that love is a romantic feeling. Other people think it's that comfortable "I've got your back" feeling you get when you're with your family or friends.

God wants you to know that He deeply loves you. In fact, He loves you so much that He sent His Son, Jesus, to die for you so that you can spend eternity in heaven with Him.

No matter how others treat you, you can be sure of one thing: God is head-over-heels in love with you. He adores you. And He can show you how to love others, even when they've hurt you.

And now we have these three: faith and hope and love, but the greatest of these is love.
1 CORINTHIANS 13:13

I love the Lord, because He hears my voice and my prayers.
PSALM 116:1

Those who do not love do not know God because God is love.
1 JOHN 4:8

"I give you a new Law. You are to love each other. You must love each other as I have loved you. If you love each other, all men will know you are My followers."
JOHN 13:34–35

"No one can have greater love than to give his life for his friends."
JOHN 15:13

And to all these things, you must add love. Love holds everything and everybody together and makes all these good things perfect.
COLOSSIANS 3:14

Most of all, have a true love for each other. Love covers many sins.
1 PETER 4:8

Jesus said to him, "The greatest Law is this, 'Listen, Jewish people, The Lord our God is one Lord! You must love the Lord your God with all your heart and with all your soul and with all your mind and with all your strength.' This is the first Law. The second Law is this: 'You must love your neighbor as yourself.' No other Law is greater than these."
MARK 12:29–31

God knows what I am saying. He knows how much I love you all with a love that comes from Jesus Christ.
PHILIPPIANS 1:8

Everything you do should be done in love.
1 CORINTHIANS 16:14

For the love of Christ puts us into action.
2 CORINTHIANS 5:14

There is no fear in love. Perfect love puts fear out of our hearts. People have fear when they are afraid of being punished. The man who is afraid does not have perfect love.
1 JOHN 4:18

Dear friends, let us love each other, because love comes from God. Those who love are God's children and they know God.
1 JOHN 4:7

May you have loving-favor from our Lord Jesus Christ. May you have the love of God. May you be joined together by the Holy Spirit.
2 CORINTHIANS 13:14

Hate starts fights, but love covers all sins.
PROVERBS 10:12

Husbands, love your wives. You must love them as Christ loved the church. He gave His life for it.
EPHESIANS 5:25

"If you love Me [Jesus], you will do what I say."
JOHN 14:15

But God showed His love to us. While we were still sinners, Christ died for us.
ROMANS 5:8

Live and work without pride. Be gentle and kind. Do not be hard on others. Let love keep you from doing that.
EPHESIANS 4:2

We love [God] because He loved us first.
1 JOHN 4:19

A friend loves at all times. A brother is born to share troubles.
PROVERBS 17:17

Be sure your love is true love. Hate what is sinful. Hold on to whatever is good.
ROMANS 12:9

We have come to know and believe the love God has for us. God is love. If you live in love, you live by the help of God and God lives in you.
1 JOHN 4:16

See what great love the Father has for us that He would call us His children. And that is what we are. For this reason the people of the world do not know who we are because they did not know Him.
1 JOHN 3:1

"But love those who hate you. Do good to them. Let them use your things and do not expect something back. Your reward will be much. You will be the children of the Most High. He is kind to those who are not thankful and to those who are full of sin."
LUKE 6:35

Do not owe anyone anything, but love each other. Whoever loves his neighbor has done what the Law says to do.
ROMANS 13:8

Love does not give up. Love is kind. Love is not jealous. Love does not put itself up as being important. Love has no pride. Love does not do the wrong thing. Love never thinks of itself. Love does not get angry. Love does not remember the suffering that comes from being hurt by someone. Love is not happy with sin. Love is happy with the truth. Love takes everything that comes without giving up. Love believes all things. Love hopes for all things. Love keeps on in all things.
1 CORINTHIANS 13:4–7

Love each other as Christian brothers. Show respect for each other.
ROMANS 12:10

You should want to have this love. You should want the gifts of the Holy Spirit and most of all to be able to speak God's Word.
1 CORINTHIANS 14:1

I have to love him?
I have to love her?
But Lord, don't you know what they've done to me?

....

I don't always get that lovey-dovey feeling in my stomach, Lord, especially when it comes to the bullies and mean kids. But I'm learning that love doesn't depend on feelings. I can still love others, even if I don't feel like it. I want to learn from You how to show real love. You love everyone—even the people who do really bad things. I don't know how You do it, Lord, but You do! Help me to be more like You, loving and being kind to everyone—even the toughest people.

PeAce

It's like soothing ocean waves washing over you. It's the calm in the middle of the storm. *Peace.* It's a free gift from God, just for you.

Have you ever met someone who seems to be calm, cool, and collected all the time? Even when others lose their cool or things go wrong, this person seems peaceful.

God can give you that kind of peace. It doesn't mean things won't go wrong, but when they do, you won't panic. You'll remember that God is with you, even in the toughest circumstances. You'll trust Him.

Best of all, this peace is completely free! Just ask for it and it's yours.

"I [Jesus] have told you these things so you may have peace in Me. In the world you will have much trouble. But take hope! I have power over the world!" JOHN 16:33

May the Lord of peace give you His peace at all times. The Lord be with you all.
2 THESSALONIANS 3:16

You will keep the man in perfect peace whose mind is kept on You, because he trusts in You.
ISAIAH 26:3

"Those who make peace are happy, because they will be called the sons of God."
MATTHEW 5:9

Do not worry. Learn to pray about everything. Give thanks to God as you ask Him for what you need.
PHILIPPIANS 4:6

As much as you can, live in peace with all men.
ROMANS 12:18

Let the peace of Christ have power over your hearts.
You were chosen as a part of His body. Always be
thankful.
COLOSSIANS 3:15

Turn away from what is sinful. Do what is good. Look
for peace and follow it.
PSALM 34:14

Be at peace with all men. Live a holy life. No one will
see the Lord without having that kind of life.
HEBREWS 12:14

Our hope comes from God. May He fill you with joy
and peace because of your trust in Him. May your
hope grow stronger by the power of the Holy Spirit.
ROMANS 15:13

Turn away from what is sinful. Do what is good. Look for peace and go after it.
1 PETER 3:11

I will lie down and sleep in peace. O Lord, You alone keep me safe.
PSALM 4:8

If your sinful old self is the boss over your mind, it leads to death. But if the Holy Spirit is the boss over your mind, it leads to life and peace.
ROMANS 8:6

"Peace I [Jesus] leave with you. My peace I give to you. I do not give peace to you as the world gives. Do not let your hearts be troubled or afraid."
JOHN 14:27

Now that we have been made right with God by putting our trust in Him, we have peace with Him. It is because of what our Lord Jesus Christ did for us.
ROMANS 5:1

Those who love Your Law have great peace, and nothing will cause them to be hurt in their spirit.
PSALM 119:165

Those who plant seeds of peace will gather what is right and good.
JAMES 3:18

God does not want everyone speaking at the same time in church meetings. He wants peace. All the churches of God's people worship this way.
1 CORINTHIANS 14:33

But the fruit that comes from having the Holy Spirit in our lives is: love, joy, peace. . . .
GALATIANS 5:22

But the wisdom that comes from heaven is first of all pure. Then it gives peace. It is gentle and willing to obey. It is full of loving-kindness and of doing good.
JAMES 3:17

The peace of God is much greater than the human mind can understand. This peace will keep your hearts and minds through Christ Jesus.
PHILIPPIANS 4:7

When the ways of a man are pleasing to the Lord, He makes even those who hate him to be at peace with him.
PROVERBS 16:7

Lying is in the heart of those who plan what is bad, but those who plan peace have joy.
PROVERBS 12:20

Pray for kings and all others who are in power over us so we might live quiet God-like lives in peace.
1 TIMOTHY 2:2

"See, God saves me. I will trust and not be afraid. For the Lord God is my strength and song. And He has become the One Who saves me."
ISAIAH 12:2

Work for the things that make peace and help each other become stronger Christians.
ROMANS 14:19

The Lord will give strength to His people. The Lord will give His people peace.
PSALM 29:11

Then my people will live in a place of peace, in safe homes, and in quiet resting places.
ISAIAH 32:18

So put away all pride from yourselves. You are standing under the powerful hand of God. At the right time He will lift you up. Give all your worries to Him because He cares for you.
1 PETER 5:6–7

Keep on doing all the things you learned and received and heard from me. Do the things you saw me do. Then the God Who gives peace will be with you.
PHILIPPIANS 4:9

I need it, Lord!
Send it like ocean waves to wash over me.
Peace, peace. . .
Can I have some, pretty please?

. . . .

Lord, sometimes I get worked up. I get mad. I feel like a shaken-up soda about to bust out of its can. That's why I need You so much. When I'm angry, when my feelings are hurt, when I'm ready to kick that bully in the shins, You sweep in and give me peace. It flows over me and I calm down right away. It's like a miracle, Father. Really, truly. . .a miracle. Your peace changes everything. I can think better. I made better decisions. I'm a better person as long as I'm filled with Your peace.

PeeR PReSSURe

You don't mean to go along with the crowd. You want to be your own person. But sometimes it's hard not to get swept up in their gossip. Right?

Your friends are making fun of that new kid. Again. You see the pain in his eyes. You want to go against the crowd and be his friend, but you're nervous, so you keep your mouth shut.

Sure, you don't make fun of him like the others are doing, but you're not helping the situation, either. Why? *Peer pressure.* You feel pressured to go along with the crowd.

Here's some happy news: you can break free from peer pressure. Be your own person. Be brave. God will give you courage if you ask Him to.

Do not act like the sinful people of the world. Let God change your life. First of all, let Him give you a new mind. Then you will know what God wants you to do. And the things you do will be good and pleasing and perfect.
ROMANS 12:2

You have never been tempted to sin in any different way than other people. God is faithful. He will not allow you to be tempted more than you can take. But when you are tempted, He will make a way for you to keep from falling into sin.
1 CORINTHIANS 10:13

Do you think I am trying to get the favor of men, or of God? If I were still trying to please men, I would not be a servant owned by Christ.
GALATIANS 1:10

Do not let anyone fool you. Bad people can make those who want to live good become bad. Keep your minds awake! Stop sinning. Some do not know God at all. I say this to your shame.
1 CORINTHIANS 15:33–34

He who walks with wise men will be wise, but the one who walks with fools will be destroyed.
PROVERBS 13:20

My son, if sinners try to lead you into sin, do not go with them.
PROVERBS 1:10

Then Peter and the missionaries said, "We must obey God instead of men!"
ACTS 5:29

The man who does not give up when tests come is happy. After the test is over, he will receive the crown of life. God has promised this to those who love Him.
JAMES 1:12

Do not go on the path of the sinful. Do not walk in the way of bad men. Stay away from it. Do not pass by it. Turn from it, and pass on.
PROVERBS 4:14–15

"Do not follow many people in doing wrong. When telling what you know in a trial, do not agree with many people by saying what is not true."
EXODUS 23:2

"For what does a man have if he gets all the world and loses his own soul? What can a man give to buy back his soul?"
MATTHEW 16:26

Pilate wanted to please the people. He gave Barabbas to them and had Jesus beaten. Then he handed Him over to be nailed to a cross.
MARK 15:15

The fear of man brings a trap, but he who trusts in the Lord will be honored.
PROVERBS 29:25

In God I have put my trust. I will not be afraid. What can man do to me?
PSALM 56:11

Because Jesus was tempted as we are and suffered as we do, He understands us and He is able to help us when we are tempted.
HEBREWS 2:18

Jesus said to them, "Be careful that no one leads you the wrong way."
MATTHEW 24:4

If there is someone whose faith is weak, be kind and receive him. Do not argue about what he thinks.
ROMANS 14:1

Happy is the man who does not walk in the way sinful men tell him to, or stand in the path of sinners, or sit with those who laugh at the truth. But he finds joy in the Law of the Lord and thinks about His Law day and night.
PSALM 1:1–2

Christian brothers, I ask you with all my heart in the name of the Lord Jesus Christ to agree among yourselves. Do not be divided into little groups. Think and act as if you all had the same mind.
1 CORINTHIANS 1:10

Go away from me, you who do wrong, so I may keep the Word of my God.
PSALM 119:115

So then, Christian brothers, keep a strong hold on what we have taught you by what we have said and by what we have written.
2 THESSALONIANS 2:15

"Good comes from a good man because of the riches he has in his heart. Sin comes from a sinful man because of the sin he has in his heart. The mouth speaks of what the heart is full of."
LUKE 6:45

Who will hurt you if you do what is right? But even if you suffer for doing what is right, you will be happy. Do not be afraid or troubled by what they may do to make it hard for you. Your heart should be holy and set apart for the Lord God. Always be ready to tell everyone who asks you why you believe as you do. Be gentle as you speak and show respect.
1 PETER 3:13–15

If men speak against you, they will be ashamed when they see the good way you have lived as a Christian. If God wants you to suffer, it is better to suffer for doing what is right than for doing what is wrong.
1 PETER 3:16–17

[Manasseh] did what was bad in the eyes of the Lord. He did the hated things of the nations whom the Lord drove out before the sons of Israel.
2 CHRONICLES 33:2

But the Lord knows how to help men who are right with God when they are tempted. He also knows how to keep the sinners suffering for their wrong-doing until the day they stand before God Who will judge them.
2 PETER 2:9

Then the rest of the Jews followed him because they were afraid to do what they knew they should do. Even Barnabas was fooled by those who pretended to be someone they were not.
GALATIANS 2:13

The Lord has said, "So come out from among them. Do not be joined to them. Touch nothing that is sinful. And I will receive you."
2 CORINTHIANS 6:17

"See, the fear of the Lord, that is wisdom. And to turn away from sin is understanding."
JOB 28:28

Help! It's a trap, Lord!
I feel stuck. I end up going along with the crowd.
I don't want to do it, but breaking free is hard.
Can you help me, Lord? Please?

• •

Father, I'll admit I can't do it on my own. I've tried to be brave. I've tried to go against the group and be my own person. It's so hard! That's why I need You so much. You can totally help me with this. You want me to be my own person, even if others make fun of me. It won't be easy, but with Your help I'm ready to try, Lord. Here goes!

PRAYER

Bedtime prayers. Mealtime prayers. Prayers for friends who are sick. Is there more to praying than this?

Did you know that prayer is supposed to be simple? It's as easy as sitting down with a friend and having a conversation. You talk. He talks. It's a back-and-forth thing.

When you pray, you can (literally) tell God anything. If you're worried about something, tell Him. If you're upset at bullying—whether you've been the victim or seen someone else suffering—tell Him that too. Of course, God already knows, but He wants you to share your concerns so that He can speak to your heart.

He does that, you know. . .in fact, He might be talking to you at this very minute. Listen close. What's He saying?

Do not worry. Learn to pray about everything. Give thanks to God as you ask Him for what you need.
PHILIPPIANS 4:6

"Because of this, I say to you, whatever you ask for when you pray, have faith that you will receive it. Then you will get it."
MARK 11:24

"If you get your life from Me [Jesus] and My Words live in you, ask whatever you want. It will be done for you."
JOHN 15:7

Tell your sins to each other. And pray for each other so you may be healed. The prayer from the heart of a man right with God has much power.
JAMES 5:16

In the same way, the Holy Spirit helps us where we are weak. We do not know how to pray or what we should pray for, but the Holy Spirit prays to God for us with sounds that cannot be put into words.
ROMANS 8:26

"When you pray, go into a room by yourself. After you have shut the door, pray to your Father Who is in secret. Then your Father Who sees in secret will reward you."
MATTHEW 6:6

"When you pray, do not say the same thing over and over again making long prayers like the people who do not know God. They think they are heard because their prayers are long."
MATTHEW 6:7

"I say to you, ask, and what you ask for will be given to you. Look, and what you are looking for you will find. Knock, and the door you are knocking on will be opened to you."
LUKE 11:9

Never stop praying.
1 THESSALONIANS 5:17

"Call to Me [the Lord], and I will answer you. And I will show you great and wonderful things which you do not know."
JEREMIAH 33:3

"Watch and pray so that you will not be tempted. Man's spirit is willing, but the body does not have the power to do it."
MATTHEW 26:41

First of all, I ask you to pray much for all men and to give thanks for them. Pray for kings and all others who are in power over us so we might live quiet God-like lives in peace. It is good when you pray like this. It pleases God Who is the One Who saves. He wants all people to be saved from the punishment of sin. He wants them to come to know the truth.
1 TIMOTHY 2:1–4

There is one God. There is one Man standing between God and men. That Man is Christ Jesus.
1 TIMOTHY 2:5

"When you pray, do not be as those who pretend to be someone they are not. They love to stand and pray in the places of worship or in the streets so people can see them. For sure, I tell you, they have all the reward they are going to get."
MATTHEW 6:5

You must pray at all times as the Holy Spirit leads you to pray. Pray for the things that are needed. You must watch and keep on praying. Remember to pray for all Christians.
EPHESIANS 6:18

"Pray like this: 'Our Father in heaven, Your name is holy. May Your holy nation come. What You want done, may it be done on earth as it is in heaven. Give us the bread we need today. Forgive us our sins as we forgive those who sin against us. Do not let us be tempted, but keep us from sin. Your nation is holy. You have power and shining-greatness forever. Let it be so.'"
MATTHEW 6:9–13

Those who are right with the Lord cry, and He hears them. And He takes them from all their troubles.
PSALM 34:17

Jesus told them a picture-story to show that men should always pray and not give up.
LUKE 18:1

You must keep praying. Keep watching! Be thankful always.
COLOSSIANS 4:2

"If My people who are called by My name put away their pride and pray, and look for My face, and turn from their sinful ways, then I [God] will hear from heaven. I will forgive their sin, and will heal their land."
2 CHRONICLES 7:14

"You will call upon Me [the Lord] and come and pray to Me, and I will listen to you."
JEREMIAH 29:12

We are sure that if we ask anything that He wants us to have, He will hear us. If we are sure He hears us when we ask, we can be sure He will give us what we ask for.
1 JOHN 5:14–15

"All things you ask for in prayer, you will receive if you have faith."
MATTHEW 21:22

"I say to you who hear Me [Jesus], love those who work against you. Do good to those who hate you. Respect and give thanks for those who try to bring bad to you. Pray for those who make it very hard for you."
LUKE 6:27–28

O Lord, hear my prayer, and listen to my cry. Do not be quiet when You see my tears. For I am a stranger with You, a visitor like all my fathers.
PSALM 39:12

"Again I tell you this: If two of you agree on earth about anything you pray for, it will be done for you by My Father in heaven. For where two or three are gathered together in My name, there I am with them."
MATTHEW 18:19–20

Is anyone among you suffering? He should pray. Is anyone happy? He should sing songs of thanks to God.
JAMES 5:13

I talk, You listen.
You talk, I listen.
This prayer thing isn't as hard
as I thought it was, Lord!

•••••••••••••••••••••••••••••

God, I'm so excited! I always thought prayer was
hard, like I had to know special words or say things
in the correct order. But it's not like that at all. I just
have to talk to You—like I would talk to my Mom or
to a friend. I can tell You when I've had a stinky day
or when I'm feeling bullied. I can let You know when
I'm feeling left out or lonely. Best of all, You talk
back! You whisper to my heart, things like, "I love
You, kid! You're awesome!" I'm listening, Lord!

PURPOSE

What's my purpose? Why am I here? How do you want to use me, Lord?

Maybe you find yourself asking questions like these.

You're just one kid in a school that's filled with hundreds. Are you special? Does God want you to do big things? If so, what are they?

The truth is, God does have a purpose for your life. But He's probably not going to reveal it all at once—He's going to tell you a little at a time. One thing is certain: part of that purpose is loving and accepting others. Treat them the way they want to be treated. Do that, and you're fulfilling your purpose!

"For I know the plans I have for you," says the Lord, "plans for well-being and not for trouble, to give you a future and a hope."
JEREMIAH 29:11

Jesus came and said to them, "All power has been given to Me in heaven and on earth. Go and make followers of all the nations. Baptize them in the name of the Father and of the Son and of the Holy Spirit. Teach them to do all the things I have told you. And I am with you always, even to the end of the world."
MATTHEW 28:18–20

We know that God makes all things work together for the good of those who love Him and are chosen to be a part of His plan.
ROMANS 8:28

For God will judge every act, even everything which is hidden, both good and bad.
ECCLESIASTES 12:14

The Lord has made all things for His own plans, even the sinful for the day of trouble.
PROVERBS 16:4

We are His work. He has made us to belong to Christ Jesus so we can work for Him. He planned that we should do this.
EPHESIANS 2:10

But you are a chosen group of people. You are the King's religious leaders. You are a holy nation. You belong to God. He has done this for you so you can tell others how God has called you out of darkness into His great light.
1 PETER 2:9

The Lord will finish the work He started for me. O Lord, Your loving-kindness lasts forever. Do not turn away from the works of Your hands.
PSALM 138:8

Christ made everything in the heavens and on the earth. He made everything that is seen and things that are not seen. He made all the powers of heaven. Everything was made by Him and for Him.
COLOSSIANS 1:16

There is a special time for everything. There is a time for everything that happens under heaven.
ECCLESIASTES 3:1

"So My Word which goes from My mouth will not return to Me [God] empty. It will do what I want it to do, and will carry out My plan well."
ISAIAH 55:11

There are many plans in a man's heart, but it is the Lord's plan that will stand.
PROVERBS 19:21

A man's steps are decided by the Lord. How can anyone understand his own way?
PROVERBS 20:24

"I [God] tell from the beginning what will happen in the end. And from times long ago I tell of things which have not been done, saying, 'My Word will stand. And I will do all that pleases Me.'"
ISAIAH 46:10

"I know that You [Lord] can do all things. Nothing can put a stop to Your plans."
JOB 42:2

[God] is the One Who saved us from the punishment of sin. He is the One Who chose us to do His work. It is not because of anything we have done. But it was His plan from the beginning that He would give us His loving-favor through Christ Jesus.
2 TIMOTHY 1:9

We were already chosen to be God's own children by Christ. This was done just like the plan He had.
EPHESIANS 1:11

O man, He has told you what is good. What does the Lord ask of you but to do what is fair and to love kindness, and to walk without pride with your God?
MICAH 6:8

So if you eat or drink or whatever you do, do everything to honor God.
1 CORINTHIANS 10:31

Everything comes from [God]. His power keeps all things together. All things are made for Him. May He be honored forever. Let it be so.
ROMANS 11:36

Do not act like the sinful people of the world. Let God change your life. First of all, let Him give you a new mind. Then you will know what God wants you to do. And the things you do will be good and pleasing and perfect.

ROMANS 12:2

The last word, after all has been heard, is: Honor God and obey His Laws. This is all that every person must do.

ECCLESIASTES 12:13

"Bring every one who is called by My name, for I have made him for My honor, yes, I made him."

ISAIAH 43:7

My Christian friends, you have obeyed me when I was with you. You have obeyed even more when I have been away. You must keep on working to show you have been saved from the punishment of sin. Be afraid that you may not please God. He is working in you. God is helping you obey Him. God is doing what He wants done in you.

PHILIPPIANS 2:12–13

"But I have let you live so you could see My power and so My name may be honored through all the earth."
EXODUS 9:16

"Go and make followers of all the nations. Baptize them in the name of the Father and of the Son and of the Holy Spirit. Teach them to do all the things I have told you. And I am with you always, even to the end of the world."
MATTHEW 28:19–20

Even before the world was made, God chose us for Himself because of His love. He planned that we should be holy and without blame as He sees us. God already planned to have us as His own children. This was done by Jesus Christ. In His plan God wanted this done.
EPHESIANS 1:4–5

The plans of the Lord stand forever. The plans of His heart stand through the future of all people.
PSALM 33:11

Am I here for a reason?
Do I have a special purpose?
Can You use me to do great things, Lord?
If so, please tell me!

. . . .

I want to do big things for You, Lord! I want to stand out, to live my faith out loud. When people look at my life I want them to say, "Wow! That kid is really on fire for Jesus!" I'm so excited to know You plan to whisper my purpose in my ear and to give me direction. I'm waiting to know what to do next, Lord. Is there someone out there who needs me? Can I help a kid who's feeling left out or being bullied? What's my purpose right here, right now? I'm ready, Lord!

Respect

It feels good to be respected, doesn't it? When others respect you, it shows that they really care.

Bullies don't treat others with respect, do they? Nope. Usually they're busy making fun of people or cutting them down—which is the opposite of treating someone respectfully. But God has always wanted His kids to treat others with respect.

What does that mean? To respect someone can mean that you admire her for her abilities or achievements. But it can also mean you care about her feelings.

God wants you to care. Why? Because He does. And He wants you to love others the way He loves them.

"Do for other people whatever you would like to have them do for you. This is what the Jewish Law and the early preachers said."
MATTHEW 7:12

Show respect to all men. Love the Christians. Honor God with love and fear. Respect the head leader of the country.
1 PETER 2:17

The person who does not obey the leaders of the land is working against what God has done. Anyone who does that will be punished.
ROMANS 13:2

"Honor your father and your mother, so your life may be long in the land the Lord your God gives you."
EXODUS 20:12

Nothing should be done because of pride or thinking about yourself. Think of other people as more important than yourself.
PHILIPPIANS 2:3

In all things show them how to live by your life and by right teaching.
Titus 2:7

Love each other as Christian brothers. Show respect for each other.
Romans 12:10

"Show respect to the person with white hair. Honor an older person and you will honor your God. I am the Lord."
Leviticus 19:32

We ask you, Christian brothers, to respect those who work among you. The Lord has placed them over you and they are your teachers. You must think much of them and love them because of their work. Live in peace with each other.
1 Thessalonians 5:12–13

But we will not talk with pride more than God allows us to. We will follow the plan of the work He has given us to do and you are a part of that work.
2 Corinthians 10:13

Be sure your love is true love. Hate what is sinful. Hold on to whatever is good. Love each other as Christian brothers. Show respect for each other. Do not be lazy but always work hard. Work for the Lord with a heart full of love for Him.

ROMANS 12:9–11

"But when you are asked to come to the table, sit down on the last seat. Then the one who asked you may come and say to you, 'Friend, go to a more important place.' Then you will be shown respect in front of all who are at the table with you."

LUKE 14:10

Then Peter said, "I can see, for sure, that God does not respect one person more than another. He is pleased with any man in any nation who honors Him and does what is right."

ACTS 10:34–35

Every person must obey the leaders of the land. There is no power given but from God, and all leaders are allowed by God.

ROMANS 13:1

If anyone does wrong, he will suffer for it. God does not respect one person more than another.
COLOSSIANS 3:25

Children, as Christians, obey your parents. This is the right thing to do. Respect your father and mother. This is the first Law given that had a promise. The promise is this: If you respect your father and mother, you will live a long time and your life will be full of many good things.
EPHESIANS 6:1–3

Those who keep on doing good and are looking for His greatness and honor will receive life that lasts forever.
ROMANS 2:7

In the same way, husbands should understand and respect their wives, because women are weaker than men. Remember, both husband and wife are to share together the gift of life that lasts forever. If this is not done, you will find it hard to pray.
1 PETER 3:7

Remember your leaders who first spoke God's Word to you. Think of how they lived, and trust God as they did.

HEBREWS 13:7

So every man must love his wife as he loves himself. Every wife must respect her husband.

EPHESIANS 5:33

Your heart should be holy and set apart for the Lord God. Always be ready to tell everyone who asks you why you believe as you do. Be gentle as you speak and show respect.

1 PETER 3:15

"Show respect to your father and your mother. And love your neighbor as you love yourself."

MATTHEW 19:19

Those who do right do not have to be afraid of the leaders. Those who do wrong are afraid of them. Do you want to be free from fear of them? Then do what is right. You will be respected instead.

ROMANS 13:3

May those who wait for You not be put to shame because of me, O Lord God of All. May those who look for You not lose respect because of me, O God of Israel.
PSALM 69:6

But God is the One Who decides. He puts down one and brings respect to another.
PSALM 75:7

"So the Lord God of Israel says, 'I did promise that those of your family and the family of your father should walk before Me forever.' But now the Lord says, 'May this be far from Me. For I will honor those who honor Me. And those who hate Me will not be honored.'"
1 SAMUEL 2:30

In the same way, you younger men must obey the church leaders. Be gentle as you care for each other. God works against those who have pride. He gives His loving-favor to those who do not try to honor themselves.
1 PETER 5:5

Do they care about my feelings, Lord?
Do they admire me or treat me with respect?
Do I treat others the way I want to be treated?

....

Lord, I'll be the first to admit, I don't always treat others with respect. I don't always care about what people are feeling. Sometimes I roll my eyes or think they don't deserve my admiration because they're different from me. But Your Word says I should always pay attention to the way other people feel. Their feelings matter to You, so they should matter to me too. Show me how to respect others, Lord. I want to be like You.

SELF-CONTROL

Oooh, it's *so* hard!

Sometimes you just can't seem to control yourself when others are being rude, right? You want to do the very thing you know you shouldn't. . .but you know things won't end well. So what do you do?

Self-control is one of the many gifts of the Spirit that God gives you.

Why do you suppose He teaches you to control yourself? If you just acted impulsively—that means doing whatever you want whenever you want—there would be a trail of messes behind you! Feelings would get hurt, work wouldn't get done, and no one would be happy.

When people are bullying you or your friends, don't lose control. Take a deep breath. Ask for God's answer to the problem. He will give it when you ask.

A man who cannot rule his own spirit is like a city whose walls are broken down.
PROVERBS 25:28

You have never been tempted to sin in any different way than other people. God is faithful. He will not allow you to be tempted more than you can take. But when you are tempted, He will make a way for you to keep from falling into sin.
1 CORINTHIANS 10:13

But the fruit that comes from having the Holy Spirit in our lives is: love, joy, peace, not giving up, being kind, being good, having faith, being gentle, and being the boss over our own desires. The Law is not against these things.
GALATIANS 5:22–23

Do your best to add holy living to your faith. Then add to this a better understanding. As you have a better understanding, be able to say no when you need to. Do not give up. And as you wait and do not give up, live God-like. As you live God-like, be kind to Christian brothers and love them.
2 PETER 1:5–7

For God did not give us a spirit of fear. He gave us a spirit of power and of love and of a good mind.
2 TIMOTHY 1:7

I keep working over my body. I make it obey me. I do this because I am afraid that after I have preached the Good News to others, I myself might be put aside.
1 CORINTHIANS 9:27

He who is slow to anger is better than the powerful. And he who rules his spirit is better than he who takes a city.
PROVERBS 16:32

The end of the world is near. You must be the boss over your mind. Keep awake so you can pray.
1 PETER 4:7

We are taught to have nothing to do with that which is against God. We are to have nothing to do with the desires of this world. We are to be wise and to be right with God. We are to live God-like lives in this world. . . . [Jesus] gave Himself so His people could be clean and want to do good.
TITUS 2:12, 14

He must like to take people into his home. He must love what is good. He must be able to think well and do all things in the right way. He must live a holy life and be the boss over his own desires.

Titus 1:8

Keep awake! Watch at all times. The devil is working against you. He is walking around like a hungry lion with his mouth open. He is looking for someone to eat.

1 Peter 5:8

Do not act like the sinful people of the world. Let God change your life. First of all, let Him give you a new mind. Then you will know what God wants you to do. And the things you do will be good and pleasing and perfect.

Romans 12:2

Everyone who runs in a race does many things so his body will be strong. He does it to get a crown that will soon be worth nothing, but we work for a crown that will last forever.

1 Corinthians 9:25

You know that only one person gets a crown for being in a race even if many people run. You must run so you will win the crown.
1 CORINTHIANS 9:24

Love does not give up. Love is kind. Love is not jealous. Love does not put itself up as being important. Love has no pride. Love does not do the wrong thing. Love never thinks of itself. Love does not get angry. Love does not remember the suffering that comes from being hurt by someone.
1 CORINTHIANS 13:4–5

Our fight is not with people. It is against the leaders and the powers and the spirits of darkness in this world. It is against the demon world that works in the heavens.
EPHESIANS 6:12

First of all, look for the holy nation of God. Be right with Him. All these other things will be given to you also.
MATTHEW 6:33

I can do all things because Christ gives me the strength.
PHILIPPIANS 4:13

So do not let sin have power over your body here on earth. You must not obey the body and let it do what it wants to do.
ROMANS 6:12

Who among you is wise and understands? Let that one show from a good life by the things he does that he is wise and gentle.
JAMES 3:13

My Christian brothers, you know everyone should listen much and speak little. He should be slow to become angry.
JAMES 1:19

Older men are to be quiet and to be careful how they act. They are to be the boss over their own desires. Their faith and love are to stay strong and they are not to give up.
TITUS 2:2

I am allowed to do all things, but not everything is good for me to do! Even if I am free to do all things, I will not do them if I think it would be hard for me to stop when I know I should.
1 CORINTHIANS 6:12

But Daniel made up his mind that he would not make himself unclean with the king's best food and wine. So he asked the head ruler to allow him not to make himself unclean.
DANIEL 1:8

Keep your tongue from sin and your lips from speaking lies.
PSALM 34:13

He who watches over his mouth keeps his life. He who opens his lips wide will be destroyed.
PROVERBS 13:3

He who watches over his mouth and his tongue keeps his soul from troubles.
PROVERBS 21:23

This self-control thing is hard, Lord!
I want to do what I want to do. . .
and I want to do it now!
That's not Your way, I know.
Help me, Lord.

● ●

It's so hard, Father! I want to control myself. I really do! I don't want to fly off the handle and behave badly. I've done that plenty of times in the past and it didn't end well. Help me control myself, especially when there are bullies around. I don't want to make things even worse, after all. Lead me by Your Spirit, I pray. I need You more than ever, Lord!

TRUST

He says he's changed. She says she won't bully you anymore. Everyone is worthy of a second chance, right? Why are you having such a hard time trusting? The Bible makes it clear—we all sin and fall short of the glory of God. We all make mistakes. We all mess up. The Lord gives second chances to even the worst people.

So what about that person who's been bullying you? If she says she's really changed her ways, you have to trust that God is working in her heart. Does that mean you have to be BFFs with her? No way. Don't get too close until you know for sure.

But remember, God is working on areas of your heart too. Trust Him to get you through the toughest things in your life.

Trust in the Lord with all your heart, and do not trust in your own understanding.
PROVERBS 3:5

When I am afraid, I will trust in You. I praise the Word of God. I have put my trust in God. I will not be afraid. What can only a man do to me?
PSALM 56:3–4

O my God, I trust in You. Do not let me be ashamed. Do not let those who fight against me win.
PSALM 25:2

There is no fear in love. Perfect love puts fear out of our hearts. People have fear when they are afraid of being punished. The man who is afraid does not have perfect love.
1 JOHN 4:18

My son, do not forget my teaching. Let your heart keep my words. For they will add to you many days and years of life and peace.
PROVERBS 3:1–2

Give your way over to the Lord. Trust in Him also. And He will do it.
PSALM 37:5

But I have trusted in Your loving-kindness. My heart will be full of joy because You will save me.
PSALM 13:5

"Because of this, I say to you, whatever you ask for when you pray, have faith that you will receive it. Then you will get it."
MARK 11:24

"Trust in the Lord forever. For the Lord God is a Rock that lasts forever."
ISAIAH 26:4

How happy is the man who has made the Lord his trust, and has not turned to the proud or to the followers of lies.
PSALM 40:4

He who listens to the Word will find good, and happy is he who trusts in the Lord.
PROVERBS 16:20

Those who know Your name will put their trust in You. For You, O Lord, have never left alone those who look for You.
PSALM 9:10

I have taught you today, even you, so that your trust may be in the Lord.
PROVERBS 22:19

Our hope comes from God. May He fill you with joy and peace because of your trust in Him. May your hope grow stronger by the power of the Holy Spirit.
ROMANS 15:13

"For sure, I tell you, he who puts his trust in Me [Jesus] has life that lasts forever."
JOHN 6:47

It is better to trust in the Lord than to trust in man.
PSALM 118:8

You will keep the man in perfect peace whose mind is kept on You [Lord], because he trusts in You.
Isaiah 26:3

But as for me, I trust in You, O Lord. I say, "You are my God." My times are in Your hands. Free me from the hands of those who hate me, and from those who try to hurt me.
Psalm 31:14–15

As you have put your trust in Christ Jesus the Lord to save you from the punishment of sin, now let Him lead you in every step.
Colossians 2:6

When you were baptized, you were buried as Christ was buried. When you were raised up in baptism, you were raised as Christ was raised. You were raised to a new life by putting your trust in God. It was God Who raised Jesus from the dead.
Colossians 2:12

If you say with your mouth that Jesus is Lord, and believe in your heart that God raised Him from the dead, you will be saved from the punishment of sin.
ROMANS 10:9

"Good will come to the man who trusts in the Lord, and whose hope is in the Lord. He will be like a tree planted by the water, that sends out its roots by the river. It will not be afraid when the heat comes but its leaves will be green. It will not be troubled in a dry year, or stop giving fruit."
JEREMIAH 17:7–8

We are of God's house if we keep our trust in the Lord until the end. This is our hope.
HEBREWS 3:6

Some trust in wagons and some in horses. But we will trust in the name of the Lord, our God.
PSALM 20:7

Every word of God has been proven true. He is a safe-covering to those who trust in Him.
PROVERBS 30:5

But they who wait upon the Lord will get new strength. They will rise up with wings like eagles. They will run and not get tired. They will walk and not become weak.

Isaiah 40:31

"Peace I leave with you. My peace I give to you. I do not give peace to you as the world gives. Do not let your hearts be troubled or afraid."

John 14:27

Let us hold on to the hope we say we have and not be changed. We can trust God that He will do what He promised.

Hebrews 10:23

"Do not let your heart be troubled. You have put your trust in God, put your trust in Me also."

John 14:1

He will not be afraid of bad news. His heart is strong because he trusts in the Lord.

Psalm 112:7

*I'm not supposed to put my
trust in people, am I, Lord?
I'm supposed to put my trust in You.
It's not always easy,
but it's the right thing to do.*

••••••••••••••••••••••••••••

*Father, I have a hard time trusting again after people
have hurt me. I'm super-duper careful around them
because I don't want to be hurt again. Even when
they say, "I've changed! I'm different!" it's still hard
to know for sure. But I know I can put my trust in
You, God. You never let me down. . .not ever! Show
me how to trust, even when it's hard. When others
fail me, I'll always put my trust in You.*

TRUTH

Some people can't take the truth. If you said to a bully, "Hey, you're a bully!" he would probably deny it. Why don't some people get it? Why can't they tell the truth about who they are?

You see them everywhere: kids who pretend to be one thing when they're around their teachers and parents but are completely different when adults aren't looking. You try to let the grown-ups know the truth, but they only see what they see, not what you're saying.

God sees way down deep, to the heart of things. He knows the truth. He knows who the real bullies are. And He's going to let others know too, so don't give up.

The truth always comes out.

Jesus said, "I am the Way and the Truth and the Life."
JOHN 14:6

[Jesus] said to the Jews who believed, "If you keep and obey My Word, then you are My followers for sure. You will know the truth and the truth will make you free."
JOHN 8:31–32

"The Holy Spirit is coming. He will lead you into all truth. He will not speak His Own words. He will speak what He hears. He will tell you of things to come."
JOHN 16:13

"Make them holy for Yourself by the truth. Your Word is truth."
JOHN 17:17

"Do your best to know that God is pleased with you. Be as a workman who has nothing to be ashamed of. Teach the words of truth in the right way."
2 TIMOTHY 2:15

"God is Spirit. Those who worship Him must worship Him in spirit and in truth."
JOHN 4:24

So stand up and do not be moved. Wear a belt of truth around your body. Wear a piece of iron over your chest which is being right with God.
EPHESIANS 6:14

The Lord hates lying lips, but those who speak the truth are His joy.
PROVERBS 12:22

The Lord is near to all who call on Him, to all who call on Him in truth.
PSALM 145:18

My children, let us not love with words or in talk only. Let us love by what we do and in truth.
1 JOHN 3:18

All of Your Word is truth, and every one of Your laws, which are always right, will last forever.
PSALM 119:160

Lead me in Your truth and teach me. For You are the God Who saves me. I wait for You all day long.
PSALM 25:5

Christ became human flesh and lived among us. We saw His shining-greatness. This greatness is given only to a much-loved Son from His Father. He was full of loving-favor and truth.
JOHN 1:14

[God] gave us our new lives through the truth of His Word only because He wanted to. We are the first children in His family.
JAMES 1:18

But we are to hold to the truth with love in our hearts. We are to grow up and be more like Christ. He is the leader of the church.
EPHESIANS 4:15

Love is not happy with sin. Love is happy with the truth.
1 CORINTHIANS 13:6

Pilate said to Him, "So You are a King?" Jesus said, "You are right when you say that I am a King. I was born for this reason. I came into the world for this reason. I came to speak about the truth. Everyone who is of the truth hears My voice."
JOHN 18:37

All the Holy Writings are God-given and are made alive by Him. Man is helped when he is taught God's Word. It shows what is wrong. It changes the way of a man's life. It shows him how to be right with God. It gives the man who belongs to God everything he needs to work well for Him.
2 TIMOTHY 3:16–17

The Law was given through Moses, but loving-favor and truth came through Jesus Christ.
JOHN 1:17

We know God's Son has come. He has given us the understanding to know Him Who is the true God. We are joined together with the true God through His Son, Jesus Christ. He is the true God and the life that lasts forever.
1 JOHN 5:20

Teach me Your way, O Lord. I will walk in Your truth. May my heart fear Your name.
PSALM 86:11

O Lord, You will not keep Your loving-pity from me. Your loving-kindness and Your truth will always keep me safe.
PSALM 40:11

If we say that we have no sin, we lie to ourselves and the truth is not in us.
1 JOHN 1:8

So stop lying to each other. Tell the truth to your neighbor. We all belong to the same body.
EPHESIANS 4:25

But the truth of God cannot be changed. It says, "The Lord knows those who are His." And, "Everyone who says he is a Christian must turn away from sin!"
2 TIMOTHY 2:19

"Do not tell a lie about your neighbor."
EXODUS 20:16

"The devil has nothing to do with the truth. There is no truth in him. It is expected of the devil to lie, for he is a liar and the father of lies."
JOHN 8:44

Lips that speak what is right and good are the joy of kings, and he who speaks the truth is loved.
PROVERBS 16:13

"He is the Spirit of Truth. The world cannot receive Him. It does not see Him or know Him. You know Him because He lives with you and will be in you."
JOHN 14:17

Send out Your light and Your truth. Let them lead me. Let them bring me to Your holy hill and to the places where You [God] live.
PSALM 43:3

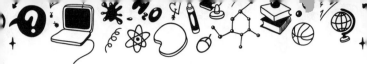

It comes out!
Like flowers in the spring. . .
truth comes out!
God, You reveal everything in Your time.

• •

Father, people don't always see what I see, that's for sure. They think these kids around me are nice, good kids. But You and I know different! We see when they bully and make fun of others. We see when they push kids around or exclude them. Today I'm trusting in You to reveal the truth. May everyone see what's really going on so that no one else gets hurt, I pray.

WORRY

It's like an octopus, wrapping its tentacles around your heart and mind. Worry can eat you up and distract you from what you're supposed to be doing. But how can you get rid of it? Can you wish it away?

You don't like to worry. In fact, you wish you could stop. But some people make that very difficult. They give you a lot to worry about!

It's time to stop letting those people have so much space in your heart and mind. To get rid of worry, you have to give your problems to God. It's not always easy, but it's so worth it!

What worries do you need to let go of today? Imagine yourself releasing them to the Lord right now.

Worry in the heart of a man weighs it down, but a good word makes it glad.
PROVERBS 12:25

"First of all, look for the holy nation of God. Be right with Him. All these other things will be given to you also. Do not worry about tomorrow. Tomorrow will have its own worries. The troubles we have in a day are enough for one day."
MATTHEW 6:33–34

When my worry is great within me, Your comfort brings joy to my soul.
PSALM 94:19

Do not worry yourself because of those who do wrong, and do not be jealous of the sinful.
PROVERBS 24:19

"Which of you can make himself a little taller by worrying?"
MATTHEW 6:27

"Come to Me [Jesus], all of you who work and have heavy loads. I will give you rest. Follow My teachings and learn from Me. I am gentle and do not have pride. You will have rest for your souls. For My way of carrying a load is easy and My load is not heavy."
MATTHEW 11:28–30

So put away all pride from yourselves. You are standing under the powerful hand of God. At the right time He will lift you up. Give all your worries to Him because He cares for you.
1 PETER 5:6–7

"Peace I leave with you. My peace I give to you. I do not give peace to you as the world gives. Do not let your hearts be troubled or afraid."
JOHN 14:27

You rise up early, and go to bed late, and work hard for your food, all for nothing. For the Lord gives to His loved ones even while they sleep.
PSALM 127:2

Give all your worries to [God] because He cares for you.
1 PETER 5:7

Give all your cares to the Lord and He will give you strength. He will never let those who are right with Him be shaken.
PSALM 55:22

And my God will give you everything you need because of His great riches in Christ Jesus.
PHILIPPIANS 4:19

"Do not fear, for I am with you. Do not be afraid, for I am your God. I will give you strength, and for sure I will help you. Yes, I will hold you up with My right hand that is right and good."
ISAIAH 41:10

"Do not let your heart be troubled. You have put your trust in God, put your trust in Me also."
JOHN 14:1

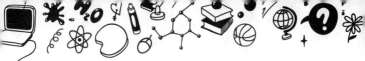

"For God can do all things."
LUKE 1:37

"Have I not told you? Be strong and have strength of heart! Do not be afraid or lose faith. For the Lord your God is with you anywhere you go."
JOSHUA 1:9

There is no fear in love. Perfect love puts fear out of our hearts. People have fear when they are afraid of being punished. The man who is afraid does not have perfect love.
1 JOHN 4:18

Do not be afraid of fear that comes all at once. And do not be afraid of the storm of the sinful when it comes.
PROVERBS 3:25

"Do not worry about tomorrow. Tomorrow will have its own worries. The troubles we have in a day are enough for one day."
MATTHEW 6:34

I want you to be free from the cares of this world.
1 CORINTHIANS 7:32

"For I know the plans I have for you," says the Lord, "plans for well-being and not for trouble, to give you a future and a hope."
JEREMIAH 29:11

"I tell you this: Do not worry about your life. Do not worry about what you are going to eat and drink. Do not worry about what you are going to wear. Is not life more important than food? Is not the body more important than clothes?"
MATTHEW 6:25

For sure, You [Lord] will give me goodness and loving-kindness all the days of my life. Then I will live with You in Your house forever.
PSALM 23:6

O Lord, You have heard the prayers of those who have no pride. You will give strength to their heart, and You will listen to them.
PSALM 10:17

Jesus said to His followers, "Because of this, I say to you, do not worry about your life, what you are going to eat. Do not worry about your body, what you are going to wear. Life is worth more than food. The body is worth more than clothes."
LUKE 12:22–23

"Look at the birds. They do not plant seeds. They do not gather grain. They have no grain buildings for keeping grain. Yet God feeds them. Are you not worth more than the birds?"
LUKE 12:24

Jesus said to her, "Martha, Martha, you are worried and troubled about many things. Only a few things are important, even just one. Mary has chosen the good thing. It will not be taken away from her."
LUKE 10:41–42

"For I am the Lord your God Who holds your right hand, and Who says to you, 'Do not be afraid. I will help you.'"
ISAIAH 41:13

I'm done with worry, Lord!
I'm waving goodbye!
So long, fears! You've stuck around long enough.
I'm ready to be all I can be. . .with Your help, Father!

. . . .

Today I choose to let go of my worries and doubts
once and for all. I'll trust in You, Lord. There will
always be bullies. There will always be fakes. But You
are showing me how to rise above them and to put my
trust in You. I'm Your kid. You've got great plans for
me. Today I choose to say, "So long, worry!" as I trust
completely in You. What an amazing God You are!